Blood Libel
in Late Imperial Russia

INDIANA-MICHIGAN SERIES IN RUSSIAN
AND EAST EUROPEAN STUDIES

Alexander Rabinowitch and William G. Rosenberg, editors

Blood Libel

IN LATE IMPERIAL RUSSIA

The Ritual Murder Trial
of Mendel Beilis

ROBERT WEINBERG

INDIANA UNIVERSITY PRESS

Bloomington and Indianapolis

This book is a publication of

INDIANA UNIVERSITY PRESS
Office of Scholarly Publishing
Herman B Wells Library 350
1320 East 10th Street
Bloomington, Indiana 47405 USA

iupress.indiana.edu

Telephone orders 800-842-6796
Fax orders 812-855-7931

⊖The paper used in this publication
meets the minimum requirements of
the American National Standard for
Information Sciences–Permanence of
Paper for Printed Library Materials,
ANSI Z39.48–1992.

*Manufactured in the
United States of America*

*Cataloging information is available
from the Library of Congress.*

ISBN 978-0-253-01099-5 (cloth)
ISBN 978-0-253-01107-7 (paper)
ISBN 978-0-253-01114-5 (e-book)

1 2 3 4 5   19 18 17 16 15 14

The book is dedicated to Laurie and our son, Perry,
for their unstinting support and love over the years.

Contents

Acknowledgments

I owe heartfelt thanks to the following friends and colleagues for their comments on various incarnations of this book: Lisa Kirschenbaum, Adele Lindenmeyr, and Louise McReynolds. Gene Avrutin, Hillel Kieval, and Jarrod Tanny also read the manuscript, and I thank them for their suggestions on how to improve its content and analysis. In addition, Sibelan Forrester, Bruce Grant, and Marina Rojavin helped me with several particularly thorny translations, and Hanna Kozlowska worked wonders to obtain the image of a group of Jews collecting the blood from a Christian youth. I also want to express my gratitude to Janet Rabinowitch and Peter Froehlich of Indiana University Press for shepherding the book through its various production stages in a smooth and trouble-free manner. Swarthmore College generously provided support so I could take several trips to Russia and Ukraine and gave me time off from teaching so I could concentrate on writing. Lastly, I owe my greatest gratitude to Laurie Bernstein, who has been my biggest fan all these years and encouraged me every step of the way as I worked on this project. She read numerous versions of the manuscript, always paying painstaking attention to content, argumentation, analysis, and syntax. I attribute the strengths of the book to her keen editorial eye, just as I attribute its weaknesses to my limitations as a historian.

Dramatis Personae

Menachem Mendel Beilis	defendant
Fyodor A. Boldyrev	presiding judge
Stepan Brazul'-Brushkovskii	journalist
Georgii G. Chaplinskii	assistant prosecutor
Vasilii Cheberiak	father of Zhenia Cheberiak
Vera V. Cheberiak	mother of Zhenia Cheberiak
Zhenia Cheberiak	friend of Andrei Iushchinskii
Ekaterina Diakonova	friend of Vera Cheberiak
Ksenia Diakonova	seamstress and friend of Vera Cheberiak
Vasilii Fenenko	investigating magistrate
Vladimir Golubev	university student
Dmitri N. Grigorovich-Barskii	defense attorney
Oskar O. Gruzenberg	defense attorney
Andrei Iushchinskii	victim
Nikolai B. Karabchevskii	defense attorney
Amzor E. Karaev	revolutionary
Evtikhii Kirichenko	police captain
Ivan Kozachenko	thief
Nikolai A. Krasovskii	head detective
Aleksandr V. Liadov	assistant minister of justice
Vasilii A. Maklakov	defense attorney
Zinaida Malitskaia Cheberiak	neighbor and owner of wine store
Arnold D. Margolin	lawyer
Pavel Miffle	former lover of Vera Cheberiak
Evgenii F. Mishchuk	police investigator

Adam Polishchuk	detective
Father Justin Pranaitis	Catholic priest
Aleksandra Prikhodko	mother of Andrei Iushchinskii
Iuliana Shakhovskaia	wife of lamplighter
Kazimir S. Shakhovskii	lamplighter
Ivan G. Shcheglovitov	minister of justice
Aleksei S. Shmakov	civil plaintiff
Aleksandr F. Shredel	head of gendarmes
Ivan A. Sikorskii	psychiatrist
Oskar Iu. Vipper	prosecutor
Jonah Zaitsev	founder of brick factory
Mark Zaitsev	son of Jonah Zaitsev and current owner of brick factory
Anna Zakharova (Wolf-Woman)	homeless woman
Grigorii G. Zamyslovskii	civil plaintiff
Aleskandr S. Zarudnyi	defense attorney

Blood Libel
in Late Imperial Russia

Introduction:
A Murder without a Mystery

On the morning of Sunday, March 20, 1911,[1] a group of children playing in the caves that dotted Kiev's Lukianovka district, a hilly suburb that overlooked the city, made a gruesome finding: the blood-soaked body of a partially clad boy. Propped up against a cave's wall in a sitting position, the corpse was riddled with about four dozen stab wounds to the head, neck, and torso, leaving the body drained of most of its blood. The boys' clothes, both those he was wearing and those found scattered on the ground, were caked with blood.

The police who were summoned to the scene had no difficulty establishing the identity of the victim because his name was written inside the school notebooks lying nearby. Thirteen-year-old Andrei Iushchinskii had been reported missing by his mother Aleksandra Prikhodko earlier in the week. Last seen when he supposedly left for school on the morning of Saturday, March 12, Andrei had skipped class to visit his friend Zhenia Cheberiak, who lived near the caves several kilometers from Andrei's home in another suburb of Kiev. Joined by several neighborhood children, Andrei and Zhenia had been playing on the premises of a brick factory adjacent to the two-storied house where Zhenia's family occupied the top floor.

Police investigators initially suspected Andrei's family of the killing, having learned that his mother and stepfather abused him and that Andrei often left home to stay with his aunt, who helped pay for his education at a church school. But the police soon turned their attention to Vera V. Cheberiak, the thirty-year-old mother of Zhenia and ringleader of a gang of petty thieves who used her apartment to fence stolen goods. According to the initial investigations, the gang, evidently fearing that Andrei had told or would tell the police about its criminal activities, killed him.

Right-wing groups in Kiev, however, were quick to assert that the killing was in fact a ritual murder carried out by Jews. In accord with a longstanding myth that Jews needed Christian blood to bake matzo, antisemites in Kiev seized on the murder of Iushchinskii as "proof" of Judaism's malevolent and murderous nature. Vladimir Golubev, a student at Kiev University whose father taught at the major Russian Orthodox seminary in Kiev, led the public accusation, hounding the local prosecutor's office to pursue the murder as a ritual killing and threatening popular disorders. Working together, Golubev and the district attorney's office sought to find a Jew upon whom they could pin responsibility for Iushchinskii's death. Judicial authorities in Kiev received the go-ahead from the minister of justice in St. Petersburg, notwithstanding the finding of the detective originally assigned to the investigation that the murderers most likely inflicted many of the wounds after the boy was dead perhaps in order to make it seem like a ritual murder.

In mid-July the police detained Menachem Mendel Beilis, a thirty-nine-year-old Jewish manager at the brick factory near the cave where Iushchinskii's body was found. Beilis languished in jail until the fall of 1913, when he went on trial for the ritual murder of Iushchinskii. During those two years tsarist officials manufactured evidence and suborned perjury in an effort to build their case. By the time the trial started, the Beilis case had become a *cause célèbre*. The trial lasted over a month, from late September to the end of October, with some 200 witnesses testifying. The trial attracted the attention of people throughout the Russian Empire and abroad who showed a keen interest in the fate of Beilis. In the end, the jury acquitted Beilis, but they agreed with the prosecution that the crime displayed the hallmarks of a "ritual murder." The ordeal of Beilis became known as the Beilis Affair, which has the dubious distinction of being the best-known and most publicized case of "blood libel" in the twentieth century. It was a murder without a mystery except for why officials in Kiev and St. Petersburg, including the ministers of justice and

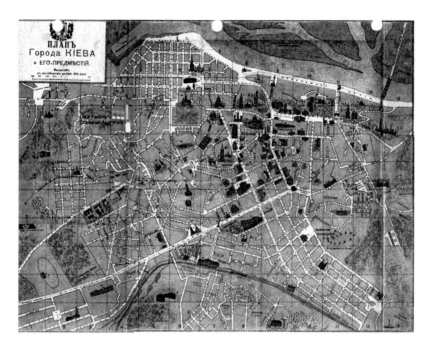

Kiev, 1911. Collection of Author.

interior, railroaded an innocent man, who came close to being convicted for a crime he did not commit.

My interest in the Beilis case was piqued shortly after the dissolution of the Soviet Union, when I arrived in Moscow in February 1992 to conduct research in the Lenin Library. I noticed a small group of protestors holding signs demanding that the library hold onto a collection that was "a national resource" of the Russian people. As I soon learned, the demonstrators were upset with a 1991 decision of the Russian Supreme Court ordering the Lenin Library to relinquish some 12,000 books, nearly 400 manuscripts in Hebrew and Yiddish, and thousands of pages of handwritten teachings, letters, and other materials that once comprised the library of the fifth Lubavitcher *rebbe* (Sholom Dov Ber Schneersohn, 1860–1920), the leader of a sect of Hasidic[2] Jews now headquartered in Brooklyn. During World War I Schneersohn, fearing for the safety of his collection with the approach of German and Austrian troops, sent the books to Moscow for safekeeping. Also at issue were the manuscripts and handwritten documents assembled by Yosef Yitzchak Schneersohn, who succeeded

Sholom Dov Ber Schneersohn as the sixth Lubavitcher *rebbe*. He took this part of his library to Warsaw in 1933, only to see German troops seize the collection when they occupied the city at the start of World War II. He managed to escape and made his way to the United States in 1940. Soviet troops confiscated the manuscripts as part of a German archive on Jewish affairs after the defeat of Germany. According to some of the protestors, Jews in the United States were clamoring to gain possession of the collection because the books and manuscripts in dispute held the secret to the blood libel.[3]

The canard that Jews engage in the ritual murder of Christians, particularly young boys and girls, dates back to the Middle Ages.[4] The charge emerged in twelfth-century England when Jews were said to have murdered Christian youths in order to mock the Passion of Christ. By the middle of the thirteenth century the belief that Jews killed Christians as part of Judaism's proscriptions had spread to the European continent, where Jews were now accused of acquiring gentile blood in order to perform certain religious rituals such as weddings and circumcisions and consume it in matzo. According to the accusations, Judaism purportedly required Jews to engage in blood sacrifice. The charge of ritual murder, also known as blood libel, gained strength in the wake of the Fourth Lateran Council, held in 1215, when the Western Latin Christian church affirmed the doctrine of transubstantiation, the belief that the wafer and wine used in the sacrament of the Eucharist contained the body and blood of Christ. According to some historians, the belief that Christians consumed the blood and flesh of their savior during weekly communion did not sit well among believers who projected onto Jews the guilty behavior they themselves felt was essentially ritual cannibalism. In the words of historian Helmut Walser Smith:

> The key . . . is the psychological process of "projection," which simply states that one person imputes to another what he himself really thinks or does. This particular psychological defense mechanism is especially powerful when a person thinks or acts in a way that is shameful to himself and his community. According to this line of reasoning, there was something disturbing about a ritual in which the body and blood of Christ was consumed as food and sacrificed to God. That disturbing element was imputed to the Jews.[5]

Church officials on the highest levels struggled with the myth of blood libel, which became well entrenched in the culture of the laity and found support in the teachings of many clergy during the Late Middle Ages. The Vatican adamantly asserted in papal bulls and edicts that Jews did not engage in Host desecration or require the blood of Christians to bake matzo. Innocent IV in the mid-thirteenth century was the first pope to take a public stance against the ritual murder accusation, and popes continued to issue statements condemning the blood libel on a periodic basis well into the twentieth century (see Documents 1 and 2). That the Vatican felt compelled to address the issue over the centuries suggests that it had difficulty stemming the belief among parishioners and even clergy that Jews engaged in ritual murder, and was powerless to stop Christians from turning on their Jewish neighbors. The disappearance of a child, particularly in springtime during the Passover and Easter holidays, was often sufficient to raise the cry of ritual murder, and if the child's body turned up bruised or mutilated, Jews would be arrested, tortured, and even executed by local authorities. Suspicions about the Jews' roles in these alleged murders created situations in which gentiles attacked their Jewish neighbors with impunity and prompted communities to expel Jews, particularly in German-speaking Europe. The best-known case of blood libel occurred in Trent in 1475, when eighteen Jewish men and women, subjected to savage torture on the *strappado*,[6] confessed to killing a two-year-old child and were then burned at the stake.[7]

Beginning in the sixteenth century, however, the ritual murder accusation began to die out in Western and Central Europe. The rise of Lutheranism, which rejected transubstantiation, undermined the theological underpinnings of the blood libel, as did the emergence of Christian scholars who could read Jewish texts in Hebrew. Moreover, the judiciary in German-speaking Europe rejected the use of coercion and torture to extract confessions, the traditional method for demonstrating the purported veracity of the blood libel. This is not to deny that some Protestant theologians and intellectuals continued to believe in ritual murder, but on the whole the blood libel tended to hold sway in Catholic Europe, particularly in the Polish-Lithuanian Commonwealth, where the bulk of Europe's Jews lived by the seventeenth century.[8] As Jews migrated eastward due to expulsions from German-speaking lands and the allure of economic opportunities in Eastern Europe, so too did the blood libel.

Recent research by scholars highlights the blood libel's hold on the imagination of Catholic clergy and laity in Eastern Europe during the

MJH 1131   Fot. Henryk Górecki

In Sandomierz, Poland, the town's cathedral still displays several paintings from 1710 that depict scenes of ritual murder. The Polish Council of Christians and Jews has offered to pay for plaques that explain the myth of ritual murder. Courtesy of Muzeum w Jarosławiu Kamienica Orsettich.

centuries it was in decline in territories to the west.[9] The historian Magda Teter has written that the ritual murder accusation entered the Polish-Lithuanian Commonwealth in the sixteenth century and tended to be concentrated in its eastern regions until the late eighteenth century. She also noted that the charge of blood libel spread to the commonwealth's western territories throughout the seventeenth and eighteen centuries, supplanting accusations of the ritual desecration of the Host. Whereas Host desecration filled the dockets of religious and secular courts during Holy Week prior to the seventeenth century, in the seventeenth and eighteenth centuries Jews were more likely to be accused of ritual murder than sacrilege.[10]

In the nineteenth century the ritual murder accusation experienced a renascence in Central Europe, culminating in seventy-nine ritual murder charges in the 1890s alone (see Document 3). The majority took place in Germany and parts of the Habsburg Empire (Hungary, Bohemia, and Moravia) as well as in Bulgaria, Serbia, and Romania, with Protestants, Catholics, and Orthodox Christians alike involved.[11] The ritual murder myth was also embraced by some people in the United States during the nineteenth century.[12]

Historians tend to attribute this revival to the emergence of modern antisemitism. Distinct from religious anti-Judaism or antisemitism, the modern variant of antisemitism was secular in content and tended to stem from developments spurred by industrial capitalism, the rise of the nation-state, and Jewish emancipation, the process of granting civil and political rights to Jews after the French Revolution. According to this line of reasoning, in the nineteenth century the theological motivation for much of medieval and early modern European Jew-hatred yielded to an antisemitism representing a backlash to the ideologies of liberalism and socialism, and the greater involvement of Jews in the politics, culture, and economies of Europe.

The prosecution of Mendel Beilis for the murder of Andrei Iushchinskii challenges this traditional division between medieval (religious) and modern (secular) antisemitism. As the ritual murder accusation against Beilis demonstrates, religious prejudice continued to inspire anti-Jewish attitudes and behaviors, even as Russian antisemitism began to acquire characteristics generally associated with the modern variants of Jew-hatred rooted in social and political modernization. The persistence of the blood libel into the twentieth century indicates that hatred of Jews based on theological grounds such as the Jews' rejection of Jesus Christ's divinity or religious prejudice and superstition as embodied in the blood libel continued to influence the thinking and behavior of antisemites in Europe. In fact, it is likely that both kinds of antisemitism influenced and even reinforced each other.[13] Antisemitism was acquiring a modern complexion, but pre-modern prejudices sustained it. Jews were still seen as deicides whose religion required the killing of Christians at the same time as they were held responsible for the problems besetting Europe as the continent underwent fundamental social, economic, and political transformations.

Moreover, the cultural and religious attention Jews paid to ritual purity and dietary laws, along with the bizarre belief that Jewish men menstruated and therefore needed to replenish their blood supply by imbibing that of gentiles, meshed with the symbolism that blood held for Christians, thereby nurturing allegations of ritual murder. The ritual murder accusation resonated in the work of some of the prominent individuals involved in the cultural, intellectual, and literary world of the Russian Silver Age. For example, intellectual luminaries, in their search for spiritual and mystical knowledge, embraced the belief that Jews had a special relationship with human blood that found expression in Judaic rituals such as circumcision.[14] While ritual murder focused on the notion of the Jews' self-interest in using Christian blood, the rise of race "science" at the end of the twentieth century introduced concerns on the part of antisemites about purported efforts by Jews to pollute gentiles through the mixing of Jewish and non-Jewish blood. Host desecration may have played a lesser role in the Europe of 1900, but blood libel still had a grip on the minds and belief systems of many Christians, who connected the murder of Iushchinskii to the Jews' fixation on blood. As the Beilis Affair revealed, even educated and sophisticated persons could hold firm, irrational beliefs about what Jews were capable of doing. Many intelligent and educated Russians did not deny the verity of the ritual murder allegation: superstition and prejudice are not the preserve of the ignorant.

Until the nineteenth century the Russian Empire remained immune from the ritual murder accusation for two reasons: the lack of concern that Orthodox Christianity had for ritual murder and the absence of Jews, who had not been allowed to reside in the empire until the late eighteenth century. But the partitions of the Polish-Lithuanian Commonwealth during the reign of Catherine the Great resulted in the incorporation of hundreds of thousands of Jews[15] and some five million Catholics and Uniates[16] into the empire. Concentrated in the western and northwestern borderlands of the empire (Belarus, Ukraine, and Lithuania), these new imperial subjects brought their popular beliefs and prejudices, including that of ritual murder, which had deep roots in those regions. Over the course of the nineteenth century the Orthodox inhabitants of the Russian Empire embraced the ritual murder accusation, though the process by which the myths about the blood libel were disseminated has yet to be explicated.[17] By the early twentieth century it had become commonplace among the Russian and Orthodox populace to believe in ritual murder.

Ritual murder accusations in the nineteenth century tended to arise in provincial towns and villages, and so the Beilis Affair in Kiev was one of the few blood libel cases to occur in a major urban area prior to World War I. Investigations and trials of Jews accused of engaging in ritual murder took place in Velizh in the 1820s and 1830s, Saratov in the 1850s, and Kutais, Georgia, in 1879. In the Saratov incident the government found the accused Jews guilty. Even non-Jews fell victim to the charge of ritual murder, with Pentecostals and Orthodox schismatics accused at times of killing children for ritual purposes. In 1892 several members of the Udmurt ethnic group were tried for killing a beggar and using parts of his body for religious purposes.[18] A higher court overturned their conviction on procedural grounds. In addition, rumors of ritual murder that did not lead to official charges abounded throughout the century.

During the nineteenth century a series of books and government commissions explored the veracity of the ritual murder accusation. These publications became a matter of public knowledge and made the discussion of Jews in the Russian Empire inseparable from ritual murder accusations. In the 1840s an influential study based on "evidence" from Europe and Russia asserted that ritual murder existed.[19] Coverage of supposed cases of ritual murder filled the pages of many of the journals and newspapers that proliferated during the second half of the nineteenth century. In addition, images of Jews as bloodsuckers of peasants and townspeople were a common motif in many of these discussions and reinforced the popular belief that Jews killed gentile children for their blood. To be sure,

Pale of Settlement, c. 1900. Gershon David Hundert, ed.,
The YIVO Encyclopedia of Jews in Eastern Europe (New Haven,
2008), p. 1312; also available online at *www.yvioencyclopedia.
org.* Courtesy of YIVO Institute for Jewish Research.

Jews had their gentile defenders, but antisemitic publicists and writers
found a receptive audience among the educated and literate elite who
embraced the notion of ritual murder as a reality.[20]

By the turn of the twentieth century the Russian Empire was home
to slightly more than five million Jews, approximately 45 percent of Jews
in the world at the time. Over the course of the nineteenth century the
tsarist government created an edifice of policies, laws, and regulations
that seesawed between isolating Jews from the Orthodox populace and
integrating them into mainstream society. Fearing possible corruption

from exposure to the Jews' religion and culture and desiring to limit the perceived economic exploitation of peasants, tsarist officials confined Jews to the westernmost regions of the empire (known as the Pale of Settlement). The regime also imposed restrictions on the kinds of occupations Jews could pursue and toward the end of the nineteenth century instituted quotas limiting the number of Jews who could attend schools of higher education. At the same time, however, the regime paradoxically adopted measures designed to encourage Russification and integration of Jews into Russian society.

The participation of Jews in the revolutionary organizations that emerged in the 1860s and 1870s and culminated in the assassination of Tsar Alexander II in 1881 reinforced officialdom's belief that Jews posed a threat to Russian society. Furthermore, the participation of Jewish youths in a variety of Marxist organizations, beginning in the 1890s, did little to stem this concern among defenders of the tsarist regime, who wanted to safeguard Russia from the travails of revolutionary politics.

In 1905 the combined forces of peasants, workers, intellectuals, and national minorities demanding civil liberties and rights of citizenship forced significant political concessions from Tsar Nicholas II. Nicholas issued the October Manifesto, which ensured his subjects the rights of assembly, speech, religion, and association, and agreed to establish an elected legislative assembly, the State Duma. To be sure, the foundations of democratic institutions and values were weak, and many delegates to the Duma did their best to undermine it as a viable political body. Yet the Duma did address the "Jewish Question," namely whether or not the government should abolish the Pale of Settlement and allow Jews to live wherever they wanted in the Russian Empire. This matter was a bone of contention at the time of the Beilis Affair, though it was highly unlikely that the government would have done away with residency restrictions for Jews. Still, the forces of reaction, most notably staunch monarchist organizations such as the Union of the Russian People and the Union of the Archangel Michael were convinced that Jews were intent on subjugating and exploiting the rest of the world for their selfish interests. Known as the Black Hundreds, these organizations took advantage of the limited political freedoms after 1905 to stir up popular passions against Jews and condemn political parties opposed to the regime as creations of a worldwide Jewish conspiracy to destroy the foundations of Russian society and culture: Orthodoxy, autocracy, and ethnic Russian dominance.

Historians have tended to portray Beilis as the victim of a government that used antisemitism as a political expedient to bolster its flagging strength, to combat perceived enemies of the autocracy, and to inflame the passions of the *narod* (common people) against the Jews. The Beilis Affair was nothing more than a concerted government effort to forestall the inevitable collapse of the autocracy through its reliance on popular enmity toward the Jews. The received wisdom regarding the Beilis Affair is that the tsarist government deliberately conspired to railroad an innocent person for political reasons. According to this scenario, government ministers, with the knowledge and approval of Tsar Nicholas II, plotted to frame Beilis to defend the regime against revolution. Tsarist officials hoped to divert popular anger and frustrations away from the autocracy and toward the Jews, timeworn scapegoats. Indeed, the government hoped to provoke an outburst of anti-Jewish violence as punishment for what it believed to be the collective actions of the Jews as well as counter efforts to abolish the Pale of Settlement by demonstrating the untrustworthiness of the Jews (see Documents 4 and 5).

Since the 1960s research on the Beilis Affair in particular and tsarist policy toward Jews in general has questioned many of the assumptions of previous analyses of the trial. For example, historians have pointed out that the treatment of tsarist officialdom as a monolithic, homogeneous body that acted in unison ignores divisions of opinion, outlook, and policy that characterized bureaucratic politics on the eve of World War I (see Document 6). For example, Prime Minister Petr Stolypin, who was assassinated during a visit to Kiev in the fall of 1911, desired the abolition of the Pale of Settlement, but his plan to lift residency restrictions on Jews ran into serious legislative roadblocks and the resistance of other high-ranking officials. Notwithstanding Stolypin's considerable political muscle, tsarist bureaucrats did not see eye-to-eye on all policies and worked at cross-purposes to undermine policies and projects they opposed. Moreover, research over the past thirty years or so has not uncovered any directives issued by central authorities to organize anti-Jewish violence. Indeed, historians have concluded that it is unlikely that tsarist officials, who were obsessed with preserving social peace, would have encouraged, tolerated, let alone planned violence disturbances that led to property damage and the loss of life. The revolution of 1905 had left indelible memories that social unrest of any sort could have dire consequences for the stability of the autocracy.[21] As the historians Charles Ruud and Sergei Stepanov have asserted, Beilis fell victim to a police force and judiciary intent on preserving law and order. Authorities sacrificed justice to curry favor with antisemites who threatened to attack Jews.[22]

Determining with certainty the motivations of those officials who conspired to frame Beilis is impossible given the nature of the historical record, which does not offer definitive evidence. This is especially true when we turn to the actions of Minister of Justice Ivan G. Shcheglovitov, who approved the plot and may have brought it to the attention of Nicholas II, who did not object. In all likelihood, Shcheglovitov hoped the prosecution of Beilis would provide the regime with the ideological bulwark that would justify autocratic principles, values, and policies, particularly toward the Jews. We are on more solid ground, however, when it comes to understanding why Kievan officials engineered the conspiracy. Sufficient evidence exists to support the contention that fringe elements on the political right, seeking to influence policies and reinforce the autocracy, conspired with antisemitic Duma deputies who had the ear of the minister of justice. They prevailed upon Georgii G. Chaplinskii, the assistant prosecutor who put together the case against Beilis, and others to embrace the ritual murder angle, steering them toward Beilis as the murderer of Iushchinskii. According to Arnold D. Margolin, one of Beilis's original attorneys, Vasilii I. Fenenko, the investigating magistrate responsible for assembling material used in the indictment, told him about the "agitation the Kiev Black Hundreds had been carrying on against the Jews and how the Prosecuting Attorney of the Provincial Supreme Court, under the influence of the student Golubev, . . . had proposed to him . . . to charge Beilis with the murder."[23] Moreover, the local Black Hundreds were "hounding the police and detective force in connection with the Iushchinskii case."[24]

Evidently Golubev and his organization, the Society of the Double-Headed Eagle, assumed that the successful prosecution of Beilis for ritual murder would please Nicholas II and generate support for the regime by providing "proof" of the evil and duplicitous nature of the Jews, thereby justifying the antisemitic policies of the autocracy in the face of condemnation on the world stage. While many conservative officials and politicians shared these sentiments, most were not willing to trample on the rule of law by suborning perjury and manufacturing evidence. The regime was under intense scrutiny by foreign governments and domestic critics for its antisemitic policies and practices, and the conspirators hoped that the conviction of a Jew for ritual murder would vindicate the government's policies and prop up the image of the autocracy. After all, government ministers and rightwing political activists could then proclaim that ritual murder was not a fantasy but a reality acknowledged in a public forum that enjoyed the respect of jurists in Europe. The jury's decision that a ritual murder had indeed occurred would therefore justify the autocracy's refusal to lift legal disabilities against its Jewish subjects. Perhaps Shcheglovitov shared this line of reasoning and hoped that a public affirmation of the perfidy of Jews would restore the tarnished image and reputation of the autocracy both at home and abroad.

The Beilis Affair provides an opportunity to examine popular views of Jews by various segments of society and explore the nature of ethnic relations in a multinational and multiethnic empire, where ethnic Slavs (primarily Russians and Ukrainians) comprised some three-fifths of the Empire's population and the "Jewish Question" weighed heavily on the minds of many intellectuals, political activists, and government officials. The Beilis Affair embodied the diverse nature of Jew-hatred in the modern era and indicates that antisemitism has a home in a variety of social, political, and cultural settings, including among people who pride themselves on their fealty to science and rational thought.

The trial of Beilis also allows us to see how the emergence of a reading public and the development of a mass circulation press affected political events in late Imperial Russia. The proliferation of newspapers and periodicals gave literate inhabitants of the empire the opportunity to follow closely the Beilis case as it unfolded. Since previous instances of purported ritual murder had found their way into print via newspapers, essays, books, and government pronouncements, it was all the more likely that the reading public was well-versed with the terms of the debate regarding ritual murder. In the aftermath of 1905, when the government eased restrictions on the press, newspapers across the political spectrum enjoyed unprecedented freedom to cover and comment on current events, albeit not always responsibly and truthfully. Moreover, the judicial process in Imperial Russia, which relied on jury trials for criminal cases since

1864, provided a public space that accommodated a variety of worldviews that drew upon religion, superstition, science, medicine, and the supernatural. The adversarial courtroom allowed lawyers, prosecutors, and witnesses to voice competing narratives of the chain of events that led to trial. The courtroom had become a forum for the clash of ideologies and reflected the growing politicization of public life in late Imperial Russia. Finally, the Beilis Affair also reveals how the autocratic regime pursued contradictory goals, with officials in the same ministry frequently working at cross-purposes.

The arrest, incarceration, and trial of Beilis aroused the same kind of public outcry that accompanied the Damascus Affair in the 1840s, the trials of Alfred Dreyfus in France in the 1890s, and the lynching of Leo Frank in the United States in 1915.[25] In all four cases the trials sparked spirited discussions and captivated the attention of their respective societies. They revealed deep rifts in each country's political sensibilities and cultural values, particularly in France and Russia where the trials left scars on the social and political landscapes that showed unresolved tensions between liberal and conservative, and secular and religious values that vied for influence at the turn of the twentieth century. The ordeals of the defendants mobilized political forces that vigorously condemned antisemitism. The trial of Beilis in particular gave rise to criticism of the tsarist treatment of Jews and inspired opponents of the autocracy at home and abroad.

One striking similarity among the Dreyfus and Beilis cases was the nature of the antisemitic imagery that emerged as the trials opened up space for the airing of vicious anti-Jewish sentiments. Jews were portrayed as malefactors engaged in a sinister conspiracy to dominate society economically, politically, and culturally. Both metaphorically and literally Jews were depicted as bloodsuckers seeking to sap France and Russia of their vitality and strength. In addition, many members of the extreme right in both countries shared a fascination with the occult and mysticism, displaying fixation on Judaism's purported intimacy with magic, blood, ritual murder, and the devil.

But important differences also existed. Despite fear by both Jews and tsarist officials that the arrest and trial of Beilis would provoke pogroms (acts of popular violence against Jews and their property), no anti-Jewish riots erupted in Kiev or elsewhere. This was not the case in Damascus

and France, where Jews fell victim to angry crowds, and in the American
South, where Leo Frank was lynched and his body brutally mutilated.
Another difference was the role played by governments: in France the
military took the lead in manufacturing evidence to frame Dreyfus, while
in Russia tsarist officials conspired to convict Beilis. In addition, the Orthodox Church in Russia did not come to the support of the prosecution,
whereas in France elements of the Catholic Church took a leading role in
efforts to condemn Dreyfus, who symbolized for conservative Catholics
the moral failings and degeneracy of French society.

The documents presented in this volume are a representative sample
and shed light on the innocence of Mendel Beilis, reveal the complicity of
officials to frame the defendant, point to the near certainty that Vera Cheberiak and her gang murdered Andrei Iushchinskii, and illuminate the nature of antisemitism in late Imperial Russia. The transcript of the trial was
published in three volumes in 1913 and provides much of the material used
here. Other documents are drawn from several sources, including letters
from concerned citizens to lawyers, prosecutors, and police officials involved in the trial. The daily press of all political stripes paid particular
attention to the Beilis Affair and offers insight into the opinion of politically engaged citizens. In addition, the Provisional Government, which
replaced the autocracy after Tsar Nicholas II abdicated in early 1917, held
hearings to determine the extent of government complicity in the Beilis
Affair. Despite the fact that it was waging a losing war against Germany
and Austria and needed to consolidate its power, the Provisional Government opened an investigation to ascertain whether government ministers under Nicholas II had engaged in illegal activities. Although many
had suspected tsarist officials of orchestrating the case against Beilis,
the Provisional Government's investigation in 1917 uncovered materials
demonstrating that high-ranking police and judicial officials, including
the minister of justice, suborned perjury and subverted justice. Soviet
and post-Soviet historians also published government reports and com-
muniqués that deepen our understanding of the trial. I have also availed
myself of materials housed in an archive in Kiev. Except where noted, I
am responsible for the translations and accompanying text and have used
the transliteration system of the Library of Congress.

The first part of this book provides a narrative account of the Beilis
Affair culled from the trial transcripts, newspaper articles, published ar-

chival documents, and several published books, most significantly Maurice Samuel's *Blood Accusation: The Strange History of the Beilis Case* and Aleksandr Tager's *Tsarskaia Rossiia i delo Beilisa. K istorii antisemitizma* (Tsarist Russia and the Beilis Affair: Toward a History of Antisemitism). I have kept the use of notes to a minimum. I have placed the documents, designed to illustrate key aspects of the case, after the narrative and indicated in the text the corresponding number of the document. At times I have used material taken from the trial, held in the fall of 1913, to shed light on the investigation into the murder. I have done so because the judicial system in the Russian Empire at the time permits me to reconstruct the course of events by using the trial transcript, which is a near-complete account of all the interrogations and depositions of witnesses conducted during the long investigation. Evidence pointing to prosecutorial misconduct was introduced into the record during the trial, a degree of transparency that apparently characterized the judicial system in late Imperial Russia. Even though I may not have access to notes of a police interrogation in 1912, the findings of that interrogation appear in the trial transcript and can be substituted for original documentation without damaging the historical record. Given the extent to which some witnesses changed testimony and contradicted themselves, records of original interrogations and depositions are recorded in the trial transcript, thereby allowing us to sort through the evidence.

ONE

The Initial Investigation

The nature of relations among Jews and non-Jews and Kievan politics after 1905 will shed light on why antisemites wanted the authorities to treat the murder of Andrei Iushchinskii as a case of ritual murder. By the turn of the twentieth century, Kiev, the historic cradle of Christianity in the Russian Empire, was a major industrial and commercial center. In 1859 the Imperial government began permitting Jews to settle freely in Kiev. Until then the presence of Jews in the city had been limited, but Tsar Alexander II, who took the throne in 1855, issued a series of decrees opening up the city to Jewish merchants, artisans, and soldiers who had completed their military service. The number of Jews living and working in Kiev exploded in the half century after 1859 due to the migration of Jews from areas surrounding Kiev. Whereas several thousand Jews lived in Kiev in 1864, at the time of the Beilis trial the police recorded some 58,000 Jews residing there, or about 12 percent of the city's total population.[1] Most Kievan Jews eked out meager livings as shopkeepers, workers, and traders, but some Jews managed to amass fortunes as factory owners, merchants, and financiers.

Like cities elsewhere in the Pale of Settlement, Kiev was not spared the ethnic, social, and political strife that characterized most urban centers. Tensions between Jews and non-Jews could run high, especially during times of political crisis: pogroms rocked the city in 1881 and 1905, resulting in significant property damage, injuries, and loss of life. Kiev also experienced the proliferation of political organizations: in the quarter century before 1914 revolutionaries, liberals, and nationalists were active, vying for adherents and challenging tsarist authority. This was particularly so during 1905 when workers, peasants, students, and nationalists challenged the established order throughout the Russian Empire.

Political democratization and mass politics in Kiev after 1905, however, did not result in a shared commitment to civic equality and tolerance. Relations between Jews and non-Jews remained tense in the post-1905 period: from 1908 to 1911 Jewish newspapers reported that members of the Union of the Russian People were acting as vigilantes, roaming the streets of Kiev and beating up Jews.[2] Right-wing political activists and organizations, in the words of historian Faith Hillis, "mastered the art of mass political mobilization, capturing the city's political institutions and the hearts of its toiling masses by 1907."[3] They promoted an antisemitic agenda that frequently embraced violence and contributed to a sense of insecurity among Kiev's Jews. Unlike elected officials in other cities who sought to reduce ethnic tensions, Kiev's city council offered little consolation to Jews, who viewed the city elders as "reluctant sanctioners" of the pogrom. One daily newspaper in Kiev called the city council "a Black Hundred council with a hooligan mayor."[4] In addition, according to Kiev's Ukrainian nationalists, Jews dominated the city and benefited from an imperial bureaucracy that curried favor with them. Hence, when Andrei's body was found antisemitic activists were eager to blame Jews in an effort to unnerve Kiev's Jewish community, already wary of the open hostility of the city government and right-wing organizations, with accusations of ritual murder.

The autopsy found no evidence that Andrei's killer had drained and collected his blood. Dr. I. N. Karpinskii, the city's coroner, performed the first autopsy on March 22nd, two days after the body had been found. He removed the top of the cranium as well as the heart and other internal organs for additional examination and use as material evidence. His report, issued on March 24th and published in local newspapers the following day, contained nothing on ritual murder. The autopsy reported that Andrei was found wearing a white linen shirt covered with blood,

Cave where Andrei was found. Mendel Beilis, *The Story of My Sufferings* (New York, 1926), p. 37.

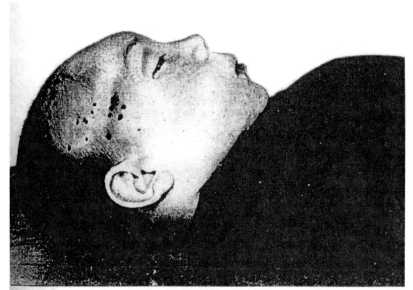

Фотография трупа двенадцатилетнего Андрюши Ющинского.
На виске видны следы 13 или 14 уколов. Числу ран в этом деле
придавалось особое значение.

Body of Andrei. Andris Grutups, *Beilisada: Delo ob obvinenii
Mendela Beilisa v ritual'nom ubiistve* (Riga, 2007).

underpants, also splattered with blood, and one sock caked with blood.
Gray clayish soil (of the kind found in the cave) and dried leaves were also
found on his clothing and body. The dead boy's bloodstained cap, jacket,
belt, and other sock were found nearby in the cave, but his pants and
overcoat were never recovered. The autopsy report provided a detailed
summary of the condition of the body and the nature of the wounds,
noting that some four dozen puncture and stab wounds on Andrei's head,
neck, and upper torso, some inflicted with such force that the object used
(most likely an awl) penetrated the heart and lungs, and damaged the
skull. The coroner found no evidence of sexual abuse (see Document 7).
It was clear from the autopsy report that the murderer, or even murderers,
killed Andrei in a frenzied and uncontrolled fashion, and kept stabbing
him long after he was dead.

Antisemites wasted no time to voice accusations that Andrei was the
victim of a ritual murder. Intriguingly, the coroner received a letter on

the morning he performed the autopsy that mentioned the approximate number of wounds found on the corpse. The letter's author claimed that Andrei had been the victim of a ritual murder. In addition, the dead boy's mother received a similar letter the day before the autopsy report was made public. Only someone involved in the murder would have known this fact, raising the possibility that the person (or persons) responsible for the murder were trying to direct the police investigation toward Jews.

On March 26th the investigating authorities ordered a second autopsy. The reasons for this decision are not clear. Some members of the police and prosecutorial staff presumably had read the letters received by the coroner and Andrei's mother, and they had begun to consider the possibility that Jews had indeed murdered the boy as part of a religious ritual. Perhaps some of those responsible for solving the crime believed a second autopsy would reveal evidence of ritual murder. The second autopsy report was released nearly a month later, on April 25th, and like the coroner's report, it concluded that Andrei had died as a result of trauma caused by the stab wounds, not as a result of actions designed to drain his blood for collection.

Accusations of ritual murder became public as early as Sunday, March 27th, the day of the funeral. Nikolai Pavlovich, an antisemitic rabble-rouser who belonged to two extreme right-wing organizations, the Union of the Russian People and the Society of the Double-Headed Eagle, disturbed the solemnity of the occasion by distributing leaflets along the route of the procession and at the cemetery. The leaflets raised the specter of blood libel, accusing Jews of murdering Andrei for ritual purposes. Even though they were unsigned, they had all the hallmarks of publications of antisemitic parties. Most significantly, the leaflets, stressing the supposed danger Jews posed to Christians in the Russian Empire, called upon the Russian people to seek vengeance by attacking Jews (see Document 8). Concerned that Pavlovich's appeal might lead to public disturbances, the police arrested Pavlovich for disorderly conduct, and he sat behind bars until mid-April when the authorities dropped the case against him.

Despite the absence of any evidence pointing to a ritual murder or even the involvement of Jews in the killing, Andrei's death quickly acquired broad attention by late April. By then conservative and Black Hundred newspapers all across the Russian Empire had embraced the theory that Jews were guilty of killing Andrei. These newspapers hammered home the point to readers that ritual murder was alive and well, and they demanded that officials redouble efforts to discover the Jewish killers. *Zemshchina* (The Realm), a monarchist paper from St. Petersburg, published an editorial by S. Glinka who took to task the editors of the newspaper of the liberal Kadet party for their refusal to acknowledge the obvious, namely that Jews had engaged in ritual murder for nearly a millennium. For Glinka there was no puzzle to the murder, as the Kadets asserted, and he echoed an accusation found in the antisemitic press that the opponents of the tsar and autocracy were working with Jews to derail the murder investigation (see Document 9).

Several days later *Zemshchina* published another editorial that picked up where Glinka's editorial left off. Ironically titled "Judaic Woe" (*Iudeiskii gevalt*—a mixture of Russian and Yiddish), the editorial declaimed that Jews were seeking to conceal the truth when they condemned newspapers for writing about ritual murder (see Document 10). Other right-wing papers also accused Jews of hindering an investigation into the blood libel. In late April Kiev's *Dvuglavyi orel* (The Double-Headed Eagle) reprinted an article from the conservative, The St. Petersburg *Russkoe znamia* (The Russian Banner) that offered an account of how Jews commit ritual murder, providing lurid details of how Jews supposedly drained the blood from the bodies of their victims.[5] Known for stirring up public opinion against the Jews, *Dvuglavyi orel* added a not-so-subtle threat to Kiev's Jews if the police did not solve the murder (see Document 11).

Despite the strident tones expressed in the organization's mouthpiece regarding the irrefutable guilt of the Jews, Grigorii Vishnevskii, editor of *Dvuglavyi orel,* appealed to his readers to remain calm. In the same issue that carried the article from *Russkoe znamia,* he cautioned Kievans to not take matters into their own hands out of frustration with the slow pace of the investigation. As staunch supporters of the tsar, they should "have faith in the representatives of tsarist power" and not succumb to appeals by people acting irresponsibly in their calls to avenge the death of Andrei with violence (see Document 12).

Charges of ritual murder were reinforced when State Duma deputies representing the antisemitic right conducted an interpellation (the practice of parliamentarians asking government ministers to respond to formal questions) in late April. They inquired of a representative from the ministry of justice whether the government was aware of the "use of Christian blood" by Jews for religious purposes, and claimed that "a criminal sect of Jews" had murdered Andrei. What, the interpellators asked, was the government doing to find the killers? Grigorii G. Zamyslovskii, a State Duma deputy who would later join the prosecution of Beilis, asserted that officials were succumbing to pressure from the Jewish community to cover up evidence[6] (see Document 13). Zamyslovskii was joined by Vladimir M. Purishkevich, a founder of the Union of the Russian People who used the State Duma rostrum to deliver emotional screeds against perceived threats to the monarchy (see Document 14). In response to the challenge posed by Zamylslovskii and Purishkevich, an official from the ministry of justice simply stated that the government was doing all it could to solve the murder. He requested that the State Duma remain patient, urging the deputies to give the government time to do its work and find the guilty party (see Document 15).

Not all conservative newspapers shared the views expressed by Zamyslovskii, Purishkevich, and Black Hundred organizations; the divide between conservative and progressive forces, was porous when it came to the issue of ritual murder. In May 1911 *Kievlianin* (The Kievan), a paper known for its anti-Jewish views, went on public record denying the veracity of the blood libel by pointing out the lack of concrete evidence over the centuries that Jews engage in ritual murder (see Document 16). Until the trial two-and-a-half years later *Kievlianin* joined the ranks of liberal and progressive voices in the Russian Empire that took a public stance against the scurrilous charges against Jews and the prosecution of Beilis. Dmitrii Pikhno, editor of *Kievlianin,* and Vasili Shulgin, son of the paper's founder, were antisemites and arch-conservatives whose positions regarding ritual murder and Beilis confounded their political allies. Pikhno and Shulgin unequivocally rejected efforts to use the unfounded belief in ritual murder for political purposes and published exposés of police malfeasance in the case. As Shulgin wrote in his memoirs, "To convict a Jew of ritual murder in the face of such paltry evidence was not only unethical but stupid. And it is useless to plead stupidity, and say it was not we who disgraced themselves before the world. . . ."[7] Shulgin believed that a ritual murder trial, which he was sure the government would lose, would harm the reputation of the monarchy.[8]

Vera Cheberiak. *Al'bom "Delo Beilisa" v risunkakh i fotografiiakh* (Kiev, 1913).

The police in Kiev were under intense pressure and scrutiny to solve the crime, especially after the countrywide press picked up the story. Detective Evgenii F. Mishchuk was the police official who investigated the murder from the time the body was discovered until early May. During

Cheberiak House. *Al'bom "Delo Beilisa" v risunkakh i fotografiiakh* (Kiev, 1913).

this period Mishchuk first turned his attention to Andrei's family because a rumor held that the dead boy was the beneficiary of a trust fund left to him by his biological father. The police detained the boy's mother (who cleaned homes and sold fruits and vegetables to help make ends meet), stepfather (who worked as a bookbinder), and grandmother, but released them after two weeks of interrogation because they had airtight alibis and it was determined that no trust fund existed.[9] Mishchuk, who refused to countenance that a ritual murder had occurred, then turned his sights on Vera Cheberiak. He looked into her affairs because of her shady reputation as the leader of a gang of thieves and a fence of stolen goods. A rash of burglaries in Kiev had been frustrating the police for several months before the murder, with evidence pointing to Cheberiak as the guilty party. The police had in fact raided her apartment on March 10th, two days before Andrei disappeared and was presumably murdered, but they found no contraband and did not arrest her.

In early May Geogii G. Chaplinskii, a prosecutor in Kiev who had been appointed to head the investigation by Minister of Justice Shcheglovitov in mid-April, removed Mishchuk from the case. Chaplinskii was aware that antisemitic State Duma deputies were monitoring the investigation, and he also wished to placate local antisemites who wanted to divert attention away from Vera Cheberiak, a member of the Black

Hundreds. Chaplinskii accused Mishchuk of tampering with evidence and obstructing justice, trumped-up charges for which Mishchuk served three months in prison. It is difficult to gauge Chaplinskii's motivations for dismissing Mishchuk's findings and embracing the belief that a ritual murder had occurred. He may have done so because he sincerely believed Jews killed gentile youths for their blood, or he may have done so to facilitate his rise through the judicial bureaucracy by currying favor with his superiors who he assumed would appreciate his efforts to frame a Jew. Most likely he wanted to placate antisemites who claimed that failure to bring a case against a Jew would trigger anti-Jewish riots.

In particular, Chaplinskii was responding to the invectives of Vladimir Golubev, a university student active in the Society of the Double-Headed Eagle, who had emerged as the outspoken leader of those Kievans claiming that Jews had killed Andrei as part of a religious ritual. Not only did Golubev initiate efforts to steer the investigation of the murder in the direction of ritual murder, but he wanted to protect Vera Cheberiak, who helped Golubev finger Beilis as the killer. Indeed, without the persistent efforts of Golubev (and to a lesser extent Cheberiak), who untiringly cajoled and harangued police and judicial officials in Kiev to focus their investigation on Jews, it is unlikely that the authorities would have manufactured a case against Beilis, or any Jew for that matter. Golubev relied on receptive officials such as Chaplinskii who allowed him to manipulate the investigation and fashion the argument for ritual murder. Moreover, Golubev had come to the attention of Grigorii Zamyslovskii, who, as we have seen, shared the student's fervent hatred of Jews. Zamyslovskii used his connections to the corridors of power in St. Petersburg to meet with Minister of Justice Shcheglovitov, who assented to the efforts to frame a Jew for Andrei's murder.

After consulting with Alexsandr V. Liadov, an assistant minister of justice sent by Shcheglovitov on a fact-finding mission in early May, Chaplinskii appointed Nikolai A. Krasovskii as lead detective. Krasovskii was an able investigator that Chaplinskii mistakenly assumed would be more pliable than Mishchuk. But Krasovskii, one of several investigators known as the "Sherlock Holmes of Russia," refused to compromise his principles and, like Mishchuk, resisted pressure from Chaplinskii to focus on the ritual murder angle. Instead, he took up where Mishchuk had stopped and redoubled efforts to investigate Vera Cheberiak. Right

Vladimir Golubev. *Al'bom "Delo Beilisa" v risunkakh i fotografiiakh* (Kiev, 1913).

after Mishchuk's dismissal in early May, Krasovskii and his assistant, police captain Evtikhii Kirichenko, conducted a search of the Cheberiak apartment with three other detectives on May 10. The police did not find any forensic evidence, but Kirichenko's interrogation of Zhenia Cheberiak reinforced his and Krasovskii's suspicions that Vera Cheberiak knew much more about the murder than she was admitting. Both mother and son denied that Andrei had visited them on March 12th, a bald-faced lie they retracted during later questioning.

Krasovskii and several other police and judicial officials involved in the investigation were certain that Cheberiak was connected to the murder. They detained her in early June and spent the next several weeks compiling evidence to support their suspicion that Andrei was the victim of Cheberiak and gang members Ivan D. Latyshev, Boris A. Rudzinskii, and Petr Singaevskii, Cheberiak's half-brother. According to the scenario Krasovskii and others advanced, Cheberiak and the gang (known as the "troika") were in her apartment on the morning of March 12th when Zhenia, who had been outside playing with Andrei and another boy, ran in. He reported that Andrei, with whom he argued about two sticks used in a game they were playing, had threatened to tell the police about the gang's activities.[10] Alarmed by Andrei's threat and suspicious that he may have already spoken to the police (which would explain the recent raid on the apartment), the gang, according to Krasovskii, decided that it had to eliminate the boy. When Andrei returned to the apartment to collect the schoolbooks he had left there, the gang seized him, bound and gagged him, and then stabbed him some four dozen times. The police were unsure, however, whether they continued to stab him in the heat of the moment or to mimic a ritual murder.

Chaplinskii refused, however, to countenance Krasovskii's insistence that Cheberiak was involved in the murder, releasing her from jail after several weeks. Suspicion of Cheberiak and the troika increased, however, during the summer of 1911. In August Zhenia and his sister Valia died from eating what the police claimed to be a pastry laced with poison. Suspicion immediately fell on their mother who, it was asserted, had very good reason to silence her children out of fear that they would tell the police what they knew about Andrei's murder. Indeed, Vera Cheberiak had insisted on taking Zhenia home from the hospital when he fell ill in early August, a move that suggested to some that she was more worried about what he might say to others than with restoring him to full health. Nevertheless, no concrete evidence ever emerged linking Cheberiak to the poisoning of her children, and their deaths remained a mystery.

When the police learned that Zhenia was near death, the detective Adam Polishchuk, who had been involved in the investigation of the murder from the beginning, rushed to the Cheberiak home to interview the boy, who had been going in and out of consciousness since his return from the hospital. Krasovskii and his assistant Kirichenko accompanied the detective. According to Kirichenko, who testified at the trial in 1913, Vera Cheberiak tried to control what her son told them (see Document 17). Polishchuk corroborated Kirichenko's testimony that Vera Cheberiak implored her son to tell the investigators that she had nothing to do with the murder (see Document 18).

Krasovskii shared his suspicions with his superiors and, having realized that Chaplinskii was resisting efforts to pursue the case against Cheberiak, complained to them about the pressure exerted by Golubev to pin the murder on Jews. Krasovskii resented Golubev's interference and worked hard to convince others in the police and judiciary that Andrei's murder was not a ritual killing. In the process he amassed sufficient evidence of Cheberiak's guilt. In the end, however, Chaplinskii prevailed and managed to have Krasovskii removed from the case in September 1911 (see Document 19). Chaplinskii turned to Polishchuk, who was heavily involved in right-wing politics in Kiev and promoted the interests of Black Hundred organizations, to dredge up bogus evidence that Krasovskii had stolen sixteen kopeks from a prisoner in 1903. The accusation landed Krasovskii in prison for a short period of time until a court threw out the charges. At the trial Polishchuk challenged the testimony of the disgraced Krasovskii, who told the court that he had found no physical evidence linking Beilis to the murder. Polishchuk went even further, accusing Krasovskii of poisoning the Cheberiak children, but the defense managed to have him recant this part of his testimony. Moreover, Polishchuk wound up admitting that all the evidence pointed to Vera Cheberiak as the guilty party.

Other officials familiar with the case voiced their concerns about the direction the investigation was taking. For example, Nikolai Brandorf, head prosecutor of the Kiev Circuit Court who had been involved in the arrest of Vera Cheberiak in June 1911, complained to Chaplinskii on more than one occasion that Golubev was interfering with the investigation. Chaplinskii, who was Brandorf's superior, warned the prosecutor that his career would be in jeopardy if Shcheglovitov learned that the murder did not resemble a ritual killing. Similarly, Vasilii I. Fenenko, the investigating magistrate, believed that the murder had occurred in the Cheberiak apartment and intended to build a case against Vera Cheberiak. Chaplinskii prevailed, however, removing Brandorf from the case before the end of 1911 and Fenenko in early 1912.

In autumn 1911 evidence against Cheberiak continued to grow. In November Zinaida Malitskaia, who lived in the first-floor apartment below the Cheberiak apartment where she operated a wine store, recounted the events of March 12th to police investigators, information she repeated when she testified at the trial two years later. She claimed that she had heard Andrei in the Cheberiak apartment on the morning of March 12th, when there seemed to be a scuffle. Malitskaia also stated that Cheberiak threatened her when she later asked about the commotion in the apartment (see Document 20).

Forensic evidence that the murder took place in the Cheberiak apartment was a piece of pillowcase covered with blood and semen found in the pocket of Andrei's jacket in the cave.[11] According to Ksenia Diakonova, a seamstress asked by Cheberiak to sew a new cover for a pillow in the living room, the swatch recovered in the cave matched the fabric of the pillowcases in the Cheberiak apartment.[12] The living room walls and pillowcases in the apartment were also stained with semen. In addition, a careful examination of the Cheberiak apartment revealed some bloodstains on a rug, but the police were unable to determine whether the blood matched that of Andrei. If the murder took place in the apartment, blood would have undoubtedly splattered all over the floor. Either the killers thoroughly cleaned the site or they killed the boy elsewhere.

Diakonova also told police investigators that she visited Cheberiak at noon on March 12th, and reported seeing the troika bustling about the living room. Cheberiak hurried her guest into the kitchen for tea and did not allow Diakonova in the living room. Diakonova's sister, Ekaterina, actually slept at the Cheberiak apartment on March 13th or 14th and noted that she might have brushed what she thought was Andrei's corpse with her foot while in bed. In addition, the two sisters reported that Adel' Ravich, a shopkeeper who handled stolen goods for Cheberiak, told them in separate conversations that she had noticed Andrei's body rolled up in a rug under a table in the living room.[13] But Ravich and her husband moved to Canada in the fall of 1911 and could not confirm the story at the trial. Nor was any rug found that supported her claim (see Document 21).

The scenario that the murder occurred in the Cheberiak apartment left unanswered how and when the murderers managed to transport the body to the cave, where it was discovered a week later. Moving a body, even one of a boy, would undoubtedly attract the attention of neighbors and passersby. People must have been coming and going all day long to buy wine from Malitskaia. In addition, the troika left on the morning of March 13th for Moscow and therefore could not have assisted in the removal of the body unless they did so on the evening of March 12th. It would have been possible for them to do so, but that same evening the troika were busy robbing a store. Did time permit them to remove the corpse from the apartment as well as engage in a robbery? In addition, is it feasible to assume that Vera Cheberiak carried the boy all by herself when it was dark? Or is it reasonable to assume that she would have requested the assistance of another person at the risk of exposing herself? Also, if Andrei's body remained in the apartment for several days, then Cheberiak risked exposure by other guests who might visit her. Finally, why did no one comment on the odor of a decomposing corpse? While it still may have been winter in mid-March, the apartment presumably had some form of heat, which would have promoted the deterioration of the body. At the trial the defense indicated that it believed the killers moved the body on the night of March 12th or March 13th, though the latter date would mean Cheberiak moved the body by herself. Along with the lack of significant traces of blood in the apartment, the issue of who, how, and when the murderers disposed of the body is unresolved.[14]

The Case against Beilis

From the early phases of the investigation, Chaplinskii ignored the findings of Mishchuk and Krasovskii that implicated Vera Cheberiak and the troika. Instead, he focused his efforts on developing a case against a Jew (or Jews) as a result of the pressure exerted by Vladimir Golubev. It was Golubev who suggested the scenario of ritual murder and encouraged Chaplinskii to look for a Jew. But before he found a Jew to frame, Chaplinskii looked for an expert who would support the ritual murder accusation. He found his expert witness in the person of Ivan A. Sikorskii, an eminent psychiatrist who taught at St. Vladimir University in Kiev. In May 1911 the examining magistrate of Kiev deposed Sikorskii with regard to the ritual nature of Andrei's murder. Sikorskii was asked to ascertain whether a "mentally diseased person" killed Andrei; whether the autopsy could reveal how the murder was carried out and the aims of the murderer or murderers; and whether the "murderers belonged to a certain people . . ." Sikorskii stated that, in his opinion, several persons participated in the killing in a deliberate effort to maximize the draining of blood from the body. He also underscored what he believed to be similarities between the murder of Andrei and other ritual murders. A specific national group with a psychological need to engage in "racial revenge" committed the crime, according to Sikorskii. Even though the words "Jew" or "Judaism" do not appear in his report, Sikorskii's use of the phrase "vendetta of the Sons of Jacob" leaves no doubt that he was suggesting that Jews were the murderers. Sikorskii clearly lacked the training and expertise to offer an opinion as a forensic specialist, but as a confirmed antisemite and staunch believer in the blood libel, Sikorskii devised a report that justified exploring the responsibility of Jews for Andrei's murder[1] (see Document 22).

Also, in May Golubev suggested to Chaplinskii and Liadov that the police should turn their attention to a "Jew named Mendel" who worked at the Zaitsev brick factory that abutted the building where Vera Cheberiak lived and was near the cave where the body was found. According to Golubev, Mendel behaved suspiciously and liked to give treats to the neighborhood children. Golubev also alleged with no evidence that the murder had taken place in one of the basements of the factory complex. An inspection of the factory's premises, however, found nothing to support Golubev's claim, an unsurprising finding for the simple reason that the brickworks had no basements.

Shortly thereafter Golubev claimed that the "Jew named Mendel" had a black beard, and by mid-July the "Jew named Mendel" who had a "black beard" turned out to be Menachem Mendel Beilis. Beilis, who had a family of six, had managed the Zaitsev brick factory for fifteen years and was on good terms with those living in the neighborhood. Beilis was instrumental in convincing his employer to sell bricks at less than cost for the building of a church school, something that the gentile owner of another brick factory refused to do. He also obtained permission for the local Orthodox church to cut through the factory's premises during funeral processions. We do not know why Golubev decided to target Beilis, an upstanding member of the community, as the murderer of Andrei. Perhaps it was Beilis's visibility in the neighborhood that brought him to the attention of Golubev. But he could not have found a more unlikely candidate for a religiously motivated murderer: Beilis was not an observant Jew.

The case against Beilis came together in July when Kazimir Shakhovskii endorsed the scenario of the murder that Golubev had worked up, namely the fiction that Beilis had committed the murder at the brick factory. Shakhovskii was a lamplighter in the neighborhood where the Cheberiaks lived, but his wife Iuliana frequently did his job because of his penchant for drink. Shakhovskii offered the information in pieces, adding additionally damaging evidence against Beilis each time he talked

Mendel Beilis and family. Mendel Beilis, *The Story of My Sufferings* (New York, 1926), p. 196.

with the police. As it turned out, someone—presumably a detective at Chaplinskii's behest—was telling him what to say in order to strengthen the case against Beilis. On July 9th Shakhovskii told Fenenko that he had seen Zhenia and Andrei walking together on the morning of March 12th, this despite the fact that Vera Cheberiak and her son had already claimed to the police that they had not seen Andrei on that day. Slightly more than a week later Shakhovskii elaborated on his earlier deposition, adding that the Cheberiak apartment abutted the Zaitsev brick factory where a man known as Mendel worked. According to his new and quite dubious testimony, this Mendel and Vera Cheberiak were on intimate terms, a highly improbable scenario. Several days later, on July 19th, Shakhovskii told interrogators that he had omitted telling them that Zhenia and Andrei had reported to him that a man had chased them away from the brickworks on the morning of March 12th.

It was clear to Detective Krasovskii that Shakhovskii's story was an utter fabrication, which he confirmed by talking with other residents of the neighborhood. A shoemaker by the name of Nakonechnyi, who knew Shakhovskii since childhood, came forward to refute Shakhovskii's testimony. Nakonechnyi claimed that Shakhovskii did not always tell the truth. The shoemaker asserted that Shakhovskii lied when he said that a man with a black beard, presumably Mendel Beilis, had chased away the two boys. Nakonechnyi knew this was not true because, as he claimed to Krasovskii, Shakhovskii had told him that he was out to get Beilis, who once had reported Shakhovskii to the police for pilfering lumber from the brickworks. When confronted by Krasovskii, Shakhovskii broke down immediately and confessed that Zhenia had never told him about being chased by a man with a black beard. Instead, he claimed that the police had badgered and beat him to implicate Beilis. In particular, Shakhovskii fingered the detective Adam Polishchuk.

Complicating matters, on July 20th Iuliana Shakhovskaia claimed that her husband told her that he had witnessed Mendel Beilis dragging Andrei to the kiln.[2] Despite the fact that several days later Shakhovskii disputed his wife's version of events, Iuliana Shakhovskaia kept to her story, substituting for her husband an elderly homeless woman Anna Zakharova (known as "Wolf-Woman") as the person who told her about Beilis seizing Andrei and dragging him toward the kiln.[3]

Notwithstanding these discrepancies in the depositions, Golubev and Chaplinskii had achieved their goal of connecting a specific Jew to the disappearance and murder of Andrei. So confident was Chaplinskii that, on the very day Shakhovskii claimed he had seen Beilis drag Andrei toward the kiln, he visited Minister of Justice Shcheglovitov, who was vacationing at his estate not far from Kiev, and received permission to pursue the case. From Shcheglovitov's summer home Chaplinskii telegrammed his office in Kiev and inquired whether Beilis was in custody, suggesting he had left the city confident that Beilis would be detained. Evidently Shcheglovitov had agreed to pursue the charge of ritual murder soon after he appointed Chaplinskii to head the investigation in mid-April. Like Chaplinskii, the minister appears to have been trying to placate antisemitic deputies in the State Duma who clamored for an investigation of ritual murder. He may have also been motivated by a desire to undermine efforts to grant greater freedoms to Jews, a subject that had been discussed in the State Duma. In any event, it is improbable that he believed in ritual murder, and it is certain that he knew the case against Beilis was fabricated. He may have agreed to support Chaplinskii's handling of the case in order to demonstrate the purported evil nature of Jews and Judaism, thereby providing much-needed ideological ballast to shore up the autocratic regime that was suffering from the ineffectual leadership and guidance of Tsar Nicholas II. After all, this was a regime whose secret police launched the notorious forgery, *The Protocols of the Elders of Zion*, for similar purposes. As the historian Hans Rogger speculated nearly a half century ago, the tsarist regime

> had only anti-Semitism and the notion of universal evil, with the Jews as its carriers, to make sense of a world that was escaping their control and their intellectual grasp. To give visible proof that ritual murder had been committed would confirm such a version of events, give it body and reality. The very monstrosity of the fiction made it particularly appropriate to such a purpose, for the degree of its acceptance would be a test of the degree to which a myth might serve to inspire, to test and to cement loyalty to the creators of the fiction and of the myth.[4]

Shcheglovitov knew that Jews did not slaughter gentile children.[5] But he nonetheless supported Chaplinskii and conspired with other officials to blame Jews for Andrei's murder because he believed it would aid the survival of autocratic Russia.

In Chaplinskii's absence the police had not detained Beilis. Only after Chaplinskii's return to the city did the authorities act. In the early hours of July 22nd, in a gratuitous display of police power, fifteen gendarmes, acting under the instructions of Chaplinskii, barged into the Beilis home at 3 AM, searched the premises, and then hauled Beilis and his nine-year-old son off to jail. They held the boy for two days, but Beilis remained in custody until his acquittal nearly twenty-eight months later. The overwhelming display of muscle is difficult to understand. After all, what did the gendarmes have to fear from Beilis, a clerk who had never been in trouble with the law? Kievan authorities asserted that they had detained Beilis in the interest of state security: perhaps they worried that the detention of a Jew for the murder of Andrei would trigger a pogrom when news of the detention leaked out. In that case, a display of force would serve as a deterrent. But why anxiety about possible unrest required the detention of Beilis's son is hard to fathom.

Now that Beilis was in police custody, which was not the same as being under arrest, the investigation of the murder entered its second phase, with the shifting of the criminal investigation from the police to judiciary. The police collected evidence and questioned witnesses, and had the authority to hold in custody persons suspected of being linked to a crime. But it was the local prosecutor or district attorney who could order the arrest of suspects. Once the arrest took place, the office of the district attorney would begin the judicial inquiry and could issue orders to the police working on the case. Then the prosecution assembled evidence for an indictment, which had to be approved by a panel of judges who had to rule whether sufficient grounds existed to bring the case to trial.

The district attorney issued an arrest warrant for Beilis in August, a sign that the government believed it had credible evidence against him. Russian law did not permit a person under arrest to have contact with anyone or to consult with legal counsel until indictment. In December Aron Beilis asked judicial authorities for permission to meet with his brother. He also wanted to make sure that Mendel Beilis had received two letters sent in November about possible defense strategies (see Document 23). The Circuit Court denied the request, and hence, from the time of his detention in July 1911 until his indictment in January 1912, Mendel Beilis languished in his cell, cut off from family and friends, and unable to take steps to prove his innocence. In his memoirs Beilis described the harsh conditions of prison life (see Document 24).

In November Beilis faced more problems when Ivan Kozachenko, a convicted thief the police placed in Beilis's cell as an informer, told the authorities that his cellmate asked him to poison Shakhovskii after Kozachenko's release from jail. According to Kozachenko, Beilis assured him that the owner of the brickworks would pay to see the government's key witness murdered. Chaplinskii seized upon Kozachenko's report, notifying Shcheglovitov about the prosecution's new and incriminating evidence. Chaplinskii conveniently neglected to inform the minister of justice that Kozachenko had already retracted his story, which was a complete fabrication. Chaplinskii even proceeded to introduce this damaged testimony at the trial two years later and made sure that Kozachenko was unavailable for cross-examination by the defense attorneys. Perhaps the most surprising element of this episode is that no one involved in the case mentioned that Beilis could not have known about Shakhovskii's depositions, which had not yet been made public in November 1911 and were the supposed reason for Beilis wanting to silence the lamplighter. Chaplinskii, however, would have known about Shakhovskii's testimony, since he had been involved in creating the lies it contained.

More damaging evidence against Beilis came to light in December 1911 when Vasilii Cheberiak, Zhenia's father, informed the authorities that his son had told him prior to his death that Beilis had chased him and Andrei from the brick factory several days before Andrei disappeared. At the trial the defense attorneys underscored the unreliability of Vasilii Cheberiak's testimony and intimated that his wife had forced him to make this statement.

In January 1912 the government officially indicted Beilis for the murder of Andrei. The trial was scheduled to begin in May, but several police and judicial officials, some of whom had earlier gone on the record against pursuing the ritual murder charge, now protested the lack of credible evidence against Beilis in a flurry of telegrams and letters to their superiors. They asserted that the case against Beilis was so weak that an acquittal was a foregone conclusion. In February 1912 Colonel Aleksandr F. Shredel, head of the gendarmes[6] in Kiev Province, wrote to the assistant director of the Department of Police that the evidence against Beilis was flimsy. He criticized the government for rushing ahead with what he believed were biased and one-sided arguments, and urged the government to focus on Cheberiak and her gang as the real culprits. He also speculated that the gang killed Andrei because of what he knew about their illegal activities. The following month Shredel reiterated what he had written in February, and he also questioned the reliability of the depositions of the Shakhovskiis (see Documents 25 and 26).

Not surprisingly, the indictment, along with the accompanying evidence, stirred the interest of the public. In particular, Ivan Sikorskii's deposition spurred outrage at the ritual murder accusation, intensifying scrutiny of Tsar Nicholas II and his administration. Medical experts in the Russian Empire were quick to mobilize and issue blistering attacks on Sikorskii. The Kharkov Medical Society, for example, considered it "shameful and degrading to the high standards of a physician to display racial and religious intolerance and to attempt to base the possibility of 'ritual murders' on pseudo-scientific arguments."[7] The eminent forensic psychiatrist Vladimir P. Serbskii ridiculed Sikorskii for violating norms of scientific inquiry and drew upon his own expertise in the new fields of anthropology, psychology, psychiatry, criminology, and forensic medicine to demonstrate the importance of contemporary science for solving the murder of Iushchinskii (see Document 27).

News of the arrest and indictment of a Jew for ritual murder also provoked a vociferous response in Western Europe, England, and the United States. Generally speaking, these responses addressed the accusation of ritual murder rather than the alleged guilt of Beilis, labeling the charge a product of ignorance, superstition, and prejudice. The protests also noted that the charge of "blood libel" had historically led to violence against Jews. In March 1912 prominent educators, politicians, theologians, and church dignitaries in Germany lodged a protest, decrying the chimera of blood libel for which no credible evidence had ever been produced. It was especially important for clerics and theologians to dissociate themselves from the views and policies of the tsarist government in order to demonstrate that not all Christians believed in the ritual murder accusation. Likewise, some 200 English clergy, theologians, judges, journalists, professors, and members of Parliament, all non-Jews, signed a protest that appeared in the May 6, 1912, issue of the *London Times*. Like the German appeal, the English protest would be republished on the eve of the trial in 1913 (see Document 28).

The author, journalist, and political activist Vladimir Korolenko penned the best-known protest by an eminent Russian. His "To the Russian Public," first published in October 1911, was reprinted in many newspapers and journals and heightened public awareness of the government's effort to prosecute Beilis. "To the Russian Public" was the equivalent of Émile Zola's *J'Accuse,* which publicized the miscarriage of justice in the case of Alfred Dreyfus. Korolenko stimulated public sympathy for Beilis by linking the persecution of Jews in the twentieth century to the victimization of early Christians in Roman times. He appealed for people to use their reason and faith to reject the ritual murder accusation. Several hundred people, a "who's who" of late Imperial Russia's literary, academic, and intellectual luminaries, signed his appeal in order to exert pressure on the government (see Document 29).

Soon after the arrest of Beilis, a group of prominent Jews met to figure out how to help the Beilis family. Led by the lawyer Arnold D. Margolin, the unofficial defense team decided to carry out its own investigation of the murder. Margolin asked Fenenko to assist in the investigation, which was illegal and a conflict of interest for a judicial investigator who had been involved in the case. But given his frustration with the direction Chaplinskii had taken the investigation, Fenenko agreed to lend his expertise to help Beilis. Margolin also contacted Stepan Brazul'-Brush-kovskii, a journalist who had been looking into the murder since the summer. In the fall of 1911 Brazul'-Brushkovskii decided that Vera Cheberiak held the key to the murder, and he began wining and dining her in order to find out what she knew. At first Brazul'-Brushkovskii accepted at face value what Cheberiak told him, ignoring warnings from colleagues and other investigators that she was a habitual liar who was using him to deflect suspicion away from herself and onto Beilis.

In late November or early December 1911 Cheberiak told the journalist that someone involved in the murder was living in the city of Kharkov and suggested that the two of them go there in order to find out more. Brazul'-Brushkovskii then invited Margolin, who was going to Kharkov on unrelated business, to meet with Cheberiak. He promised the lawyer that someone with important information about the murder would meet with the three of them and reveal details about the case. But Cheberiak had nothing to tell Margolin that he did not already know and did not take them to meet the mystery person. Realizing that Cheberiak had played him for a fool, Brazul'-Brushkovskii returned to Kiev and joined forces with Krasovskii, the disgraced detective. The journalist became determined to expose Cheberiak's involvement, and he published a series of articles in the liberal-leaning *Kievskaia mysl'* (Kievan Thought) that accused Cheberiak and her gang of the murder.[8] He received support from an unexpected quarter when *Kievlianin* supported Brazul'-Brushkovskii's accusation that government prosecutors were ignoring evidence that pointed to the guilt of Cheberiak and her gang.

Already on the defensive, Chaplinskii found it necessary to defend his decision to pursue Beilis rather than devote resources to investigate what many believed to be a more promising case against Cheberiak. Only a few people knew that Chaplinskii and some of his assistants were working with Vera Cheberiak to manufacture evidence against Beilis. Chaplinskii's stubborn determination to prosecute Beilis puzzled many officials, and in late May 1912 Chaplinskii explained his refusal to bend to pressure in a letter to Aleksandr Liadov, Assistant Minister of Justice. He claimed that Brazul'-Brushkovskii was trying to discredit the investigation by providing "patently absurd" information. Chaplinskii refused to drop the case against Beilis just because others had been taken in by false evidence (see Document 30).

Cover of *Dvuglavyi orel* (March 11, 1912), commemorating the first anniversary of Andrei's martyrdom. The newspaper warns Christians to protect their children because "kike Passover" begins on March 17. Courtesy of Russian National Library, Newspaper Division.

Given this turn of events, Shcheglovitov ordered the postponement of the trial, which meant the withdrawal of the indictment. Consequently, those involved in the conspiracy against Beilis, particularly Chaplinskii and Shcheglovitov, had to reopen the investigation and build a new case for a second indictment. In other words, the Russian Empire's minister of justice chose to continue the charade of an impartial investigation and permitted Chaplinskii to continue soliciting additional tainted evidence. He was evidently not concerned that Beilis would have to spend more time behind bars, waiting for his day in court. Nor was he concerned with the pursuit of justice.

A second indictment was issued a year later in 1913: two members of the board of judges that had to approve the indictment refused to do so, while the other three refused to quash it on the grounds that the judiciary would lose face if the panel released a person who had been kept in prison for close to two years. The judges preferred to continue the miscarriage of justice rather than admit in public that the case against Beilis was built on lies. Unlike the January 1912 indictment, the second indictment stressed the ritual murder aspect of the case, which signaled the prosecution's decision to focus on "proving" the reality of the blood libel even when the evidence against Beilis was critically weak. Given the attention the press had been giving to Vera Cheberiak, the second indictment also devoted space to parrying accusations that she and her gang were the guilty parties.

Coverage of the investigation by the liberal press decreased between the time the first indictment was canceled and the trial began in late September 1913. The antisemitic right, however, maintained its campaign to keep the murder and blood libel in the public eye. In 1912 and 1913, on the anniversary of Iushchinskii's disappearance, *Dvuglavyi orel* announced that Jewish Passover was approaching and warned gentiles to supervise their children more carefully during what it claimed to be a particularly dangerous time of the year. On March 13, 1913, the newspaper published a large photo of Iushchinskii's corpse with the caption, "Christians, Keep Your Children Safe!!! Kike *Peisakh* Begins on April 15!" with the accompanying poem, "Poem to Andriusha Iuschinskii"[9] (see Document 31).

THREE

The Trial

For thirty-four days in autumn 1913 the public's attention was riveted on the trial, which began on September 25th and ended on October 28th. Court sessions could run long, generally starting in mid-morning and sometimes lasting well into the evening, even midnight on one occasion. Despite the length of the trial, interest in the fate of Beilis did not flag, appearing to be the only topic of conversation for the duration of the trial. Reporters from over 100 Russian newspapers and correspondents from Europe, England, and the United States covered the proceedings. The daily press in Kiev and elsewhere in the country gave summaries of the trial, with a few even printing a verbatim copy of the transcript.

Detractors of the government suggested that the prosecution tried to stack the jury with peasants in the belief that it could influence the thinking of peasants more easily than it could manipulate the opinions of educated Kievans. Given the fact that six jurors came from the peasant estate (though only one farmed) and, according to one account, ten of the twelve jurors had only elementary school educations, there may be some truth to the accusation.[1] The percentage of peasant jurors in the Beilis trial was much higher than the average for major cities. For example, peasants comprised less than 10 percent of jurors in Moscow and St. Petersburg, even though they were a dominant presence in the population.[2]

Sketch of jury. *Al'bom "Delo Beilisa" v risunkakh i fotografiiakh* (Kiev, 1913).

On the second day of the trial, the indictment, which ran twenty pages with two columns on each page, was read aloud, thereby establishing the structure of the trial proceedings. The indictment summarized the investigation since the discovery of Andrei's body to the start of the trial and skewed the evidence to favor the government's contention that a ritual murder had occurred. In some instances the depositions of witnesses were misrepresented in order to strengthen the government's case. In others the prosecution simply failed to account for discrepancies in the accounts of witnesses. According to the prosecution, Beilis did not act alone; rather he worked in tandem with unknown co-conspirators who planned the murder for religious reasons. Yet there was no specific mention of Judaism or the fact that Beilis was Jewish. The government preferred to use the term "religious fanaticism" and then relied on the testimony of witnesses to demonstrate that Judaism purportedly required Jews to engage in ritual murder (see Document 32).

The relative transparency of the trial merits special attention because the prosecution allowed all the inconsistencies and contradictions of the

Entry ticket to courtoom. "Beilis Case Papers," copyright
East View Information Services, 2005.

evidence gathered during the long investigation to become part of the
public record. Pre-trial depositions were presented at the trial and became
part of the official record. This meant that the contradictory testimony
offered by witnesses, the evidence pointing to the dereliction of duty by
the police, the information indicating that Vera Cheberiak and the troika
were the murderers, the evidence pointing to the innocence of Beilis,
and the instances of government coercion of witnesses and suborning of
perjury were made public.

The only opaque aspect of the trial was the conspiracy to frame Beilis
and deflect attention away from Cheberiak. The prosecution was clearly
more interested in demonstrating her innocence than it was in building
a solid case against Beilis. Hence, significant space in the indictment
was devoted to the exoneration of Cheberiak than to the guilt of the defendant. One reason for this strategy was simple: the government had
acknowledged to itself that the case against Beilis was probably unwin-
nable, but it was confident that it could convince the jury that a ritual
murder had occurred. In other words, the prosecution hoped to show the
world that Jews in the twentieth century engaged in the ritual killing of

Guards accompany Beilis to the courtroom. *Al'bom "Delo Beilisa"*
v risunkakh i fotografiiakh (Kiev, 1913).

Christian youths. And in order to make a persuasive case, the government
needed to demonstrate Cheberiak's innocence.

Several journalists quickly noted this fact. The correspondent for
Kievskaia mysl' pointed out that the charges against Beilis indicated that
the killer was a "fanatic or savage." If that were the case, the correspondent reasoned, then how could the government suspect Beilis, a Jew who
did not observe the Sabbath or wear *peyess* (sidelocks or sidecurls worn
by Orthodox male Jews)? "What kind of fanatic is Beilis?" mused the
correspondent, who had the impression that the prosecution had little
interest in Beilis. For the correspondent, Beilis was on trial as a surrogate
for "all the Jewish people" and an acquittal would not "let the Jews off
the hook" because the Jewish people would be "shown to use Christian
blood."[3]

Defenders of Beilis assembled a formidable team of eminent attorneys. All members of the defense team were well versed in the law, holding their own in the courtroom when cross-examining witnesses and
enjoying tangling with the prosecution and judge on procedural matters.

With Margolin excluded from the defense team because of his earlier contact with Cheberiak, Oskar O. Gruzenberg headed the defense. He boasted a reputation as the best Jewish criminal lawyer at the time, one who worked tirelessly on behalf of people accused of political crimes, most notably the writer Maxim Gorky and revolutionary Leon Trotsky, both of whom had been accused of fomenting insurrection in 1905. A champion of civil rights and political freedom, Gruzenberg relished the opportunity to cross-examine the government's witnesses. He was assisted by Aleksandr S. Zarudnyi, Dimitri N. Grigorovich-Barskii, and Nikolai B. Karabchevskii, all non-Jews. In addition, Vasilii A. Maklakov, a lawyer and liberal member of the State Duma, joined the defense team. Ironically, his brother Nikolai, who did not share his brother's political views and affiliations, was serving as the minister of the interior at the time of the trial.

The state's case was handled by Oskar Iu. Vipper, a Shcheglovitov appointee whose dislike of Jews was expected to help the government win a conviction. Russian law also permitted the participation of civil plaintiffs, private lawyers whose role was to obtain damages for an aggrieved party wanting to reclaim lost money or honor without filing a separate suit. The prosecutor and private lawyers worked independently of each other, but they shared the common goal of convicting the defendant. One civil plaintiff was Grigorii Zamyslovskii, the antisemitic member of the State Duma who worked with the student Golubev to publicize the ritual nature of the murder. He was joined by Aleksei S. Shmakov, another member of the State Duma who was well known for his antisemitic views and also played a role in spreading the charge that Andrei had been the victim of a ritual murder. Shmakov reportedly had one wall of his office covered with drawings of Jewish noses.

He and Zamyslovskii represented Andrei's mother, though it is not clear how her son's death resulted in a loss of money or honor.[4] At first she rejected the overtures of Shmakov and Zamyslovskii, but she eventually succumbed to the pressure exerted by the Union of the Russian People and the Society of the Double-Headed Eagle, which were anxious to have the two State Duma deputies involved in the trial because they could be relied on to be relentless advocates of the ritual murder accusation. Both men vigorously participated in the trial, interjecting questions and comments during the testimony of witnesses and never failing to voice their anti-Jewish prejudices. Lastly, Fyodor A. Boldyrev presided over the trial. Even though his comment and rulings revealed his partiality to the prosecution, the judge did try to rein in the more irresponsible and antisemitic statements made by the prosecution and civil plaintiffs.

Fearing civil disturbances, political protests, and even a pogrom during the trial, authorities redoubled their efforts to maintain law and order. Two weeks before the start of the trial, the governor-general of Kiev requested that 300 Cossacks be stationed at police stations throughout the city, ready to act at the first sign of trouble. He also strengthened the presence of the police, particularly in Jewish neighborhoods, for the duration of the trial. In addition, authorities heightened surveillance of right- and left-wing organizations and summoned representatives of the Black Hundreds and the Jewish community to a meeting at which they were warned not to stage demonstrations or rallies. Despite this warning, socialist students at a polytechnic institute held a brief demonstration in support of Beilis in early October; the police quickly detained them. At the university some students boycotted classes, but an appeal by Kiev's Social Democrats to organize a one-day labor strike in a show of solidarity with Beilis fell on deaf ears (see Document 33). The police also monitored the goings-on in restaurants, taverns, beer halls, especially among the unemployed and uneducated who were viewed as particularly vulnerable to pogrom-mongering. Rumors about an impending pogrom were rife, but no incidents of anti-Jewish violence were reported during the trial.

Along with these measures of police surveillance and vigilance, authorities tried to allay fears and anxieties among the populace during the trial. Officials kept a close eye on newspaper articles and leaflets that they believed promoted hatred between Jews and non-Jews. They ordered the confiscation of printed matter that threatened the social calm of the city and sought to detain those responsible for printing the offending literature. In one incident, the official responsible for supervising the press in Kiev reported on the action he took after an incendiary article appeared in the *Dvuglavyi orel* (see Document 34).

Several newspapers acted responsibly by trying to calm people's fears and play down rumors of ritual murder. The article "The Eternal Fairy Tale" from *Narodnaia kopeika* (The People's Kopek) condemned the blood libel as a myth that "sows darkness and ignorance," and expressed concern that the ritual murder accusation threatened Jews throughout the Russian Empire (see Document 35) An article in the conservative *Russkoe znamia* (The Russian Banner) called upon the Black Hundreds to exercise restraint and conduct themselves in a sensible, peaceful manner. The author, however, was no friend of the Jews: he was simply confident that the jury would convict Beilis and worried that anti-Jewish violence would undermine the victory of Christianity over Judaism and Jews. But the author's intimation that Jews themselves were hoping to foment anti-Jewish violence underscores the contradictory impulses of the antisemitic right (see Document 36).

During the trial many citizens sent letters to the police and prosecution in an effort to assist the government. The letter writers evidently considered themselves to be performing their civic duty out of concern for the well-being of society and the safety of their fellow citizens. The appearance of a literate public intent on acting independently of the autocracy and participating in civic affairs signaled the emergence of civil society in late Imperial Russia. As one person wrote, he was obligated to help the police in a case that was "extremely important for every Russian citizen."[5] The overwhelming majority of letter writers insisted that Jews murdered Andrei as part of a ritual murder. The letters demonstrate the widespread fascination of early twentieth-century Imperial Russian society with a religious prejudice that was centuries old and reveals the extent to which the literate public embraced the belief that Jews required Christian blood for religious purposes. The letters also show that the prosecution's decision to base its strategy on the public's belief in blood libel was not ill chosen.

Some letter writers referred to personal experiences as well as rumor and hearsay to provide information they believed would help the government. Others directed the police and prosecution to books and pamphlets that purportedly shed light on ritual murder. In one letter dated February 25, 1912, the author, who invoked a curious mixture of science, astrology, and mysticism, wrote that he was sure that Andrei did not die an "agonizing" death. He claimed that the patterns of the wounds, when connected by lines, corresponded to well-known constellations. He even enclosed two drawings of the corpse to illustrate his point. No signature appears on the letter, but evidence indicates that Grigorii Opanasenko, a prominent member of one of Kiev's antisemitic organizations, was the author (see Document 37).

Some letters came from people who recommended fortunetelling, séances, and hypnosis to uncover the murderers, expressing, like Opanasenko, their belief in mysticism and the occult. As in Europe, England, and the United States, occult and mystical movements had wide appeal to people in the Russian Empire in the second half of the nineteenth and early twentieth centuries. In particular, Spiritualism, the belief in life after death and the ability of the living to communicate with the spirits of the deceased, was especially popular among educated Russians. By 1900 the number of avowed Spiritualists throughout the world reached into the millions; in Moscow and St. Petersburg alone there were an estimated 1,600 Spiritualist groups.[6]

In one letter a woman named Ekaterina Ivanovna claimed that hypnotism would get to the bottom of the affair (see Document 38). Another letter described how a group of believers in Spiritualism conducted three séances over the course of eight days in mid-October 1913 in order to contact Andrei's spirit and ascertain who killed him. For the most part the séances simply recounted what the public already knew about the murder, but the letter writer also offered additional information purportedly gleaned from the séances. For example, one of the séances revealed that someone named Zhokman actively assisted Beilis. However, nobody with that or a similar sounding name appears in any of the materials from the trial. The séance participants also claimed to know the whereabouts of Andrei's trousers and overcoat, which were not with the boy's body in the cave (see Document 39).

The press in Europe, England, and the United States followed the trial carefully. The internal affairs of tsarist Russia, particularly when they concerned government policy toward Jews and the slow pace of political reform, were a favorite topic for newspapers with a readership interested in foreign affairs. The *New York Times* published an indignant editorial declaring Beilis's innocence and decrying not only the accusation of ritual murder but the tsarist regime's malfeasance. Like Korolenko's "To the Russian People" two years earlier, the *Times* compared contemporary accusations against Jews with the Roman persecution of Christians nearly two millennia earlier. The editorial urged the tsarist government

Yosel Gruzenberg, "Well, Mendel, this time it turned out okay, but next
time be careful," *Dvuglavyi orel*, no. 44 (October 30, 1913): 1.
Courtesy of Russian National Library, Newspaper Division.

to eliminate anti-Jewish prejudices and biases from Russian Orthodoxy
(see Document 40).

The antisemitic press also turned to visual imagery to convey the
message that Jews threatened the fabric of late Imperial Russian society
and culture. Not only were Jews viewed as exploiters of the noble peas-
antry, but they were also regarded as subverters of the autocracy's political values by advocating liberal and revolutionary reforms. *Dvuglavyi
orel* drew upon antisemitic caricatures and stereotypes to brand Beilis
and his defenders as enemies of the Russian people. Cartoonists for the

"See, Yosel, this is Beilis!" In Yiddish with Cyrillic letters and in Russian. The round object held by both the boy and the idol is the Host, or sacramental bread. The knife in the idol's right hand is used to desecrate the Host. *Dvuglavyi orel,* no. 49 (November 24, 1913): 4. Courtesy of Russian National Library, Newspaper Division.

newspaper emphasized the Jews' purported worship of money and idols, and they linked Beilis to the centuries-old accusation that Jews were in cahoots with the devil. They also did not shy away from endowing Jews with stereotypical physical attributes such as hooked noses, thick lips, big ears, and bushy eyebrows. At times these cartoonists portrayed Jews as pests with human attributes.

❖ ❖ ❖

After spending over two years assembling a case against Beilis built on false testimony, flights of fancy, and willful rejection of the truth, the prosecution could not present a coherent argument against Beilis. The trial was a comedy of errors because the case against Beilis was characterized by serious shortcomings, the most obvious being the lack of any physical

Тянутъ-потянутъ—вытянуть не могутъ...

"Futile efforts: They pull and pull, but they are unable to pull him out." In the ditch Satan prevents Beilis's lawyers from pulling him free. The word "ritual" appears in the bottom left corner, and a snake slithers in the foreground. *Dvuglavyi orel,* no. 40 (October 26, 1913): 4. Courtesy of Russian National Library, Newspaper Division.

evidence linking Beilis to the murder. The case against Beilis began to unravel as soon as the prosecution called several witnesses to the stand. This should not have surprised the government's attorneys since these witnesses had provided contradictory statements in the pretrial depositions or had offered transparently bogus testimony to investigators. Perhaps it was the desperation of the government to pin the murder on Beilis that led it to place so much faith in the testimony of witnesses such as Kazimir Shakhovskii, Iuliana Shakhovskaia, and Anna Zakharova, the Wolf-Woman. Their pretrial depositions were riddled with flaws and contradictions. They had trouble sticking to their stories, changing their testimony from one deposition to the next. Adding to their lack of credibility was their admissions that they drank vodka to excess.

At the trial Kazimir Shakhovskii claimed that police investigators beat him until he agreed to affirm that he witnessed Beilis drag Andrei toward the kiln on the day the boy disappeared. Shakhovskii's refusal to answer some questions posed by defense lawyers at the trial suggests that he was reluctant to provide full details of police abuse, perhaps out

Гоняютъ уфъ одного окно, а мы увлетимъ уфъ другово.

"They drive us out through one window, but we fly in through
another." *Dvuglavyi orel,* no. 47 (November 10, 1913): 4. Courtesy
of Russian National Library, Newspaper Division.

of fear of what might happen to him after he left the witness stand (see
Document 41). He also asserted that the police plied him and his wife
with vodka and threatened bodily harm against her. In her testimony
Iuliana Shakhovskaia had trouble offering a consistent account of what
she knew about the murder, and efforts to have her clarify her testimony
further undermined the prosecution's case. Under oath Shakhovskaia
revealed that the police pressured her to testify that her husband and
Wolf-Woman had seen Beilis seize Andrei. She also admitted that the
police offered her a reward for her fabricated story (see Document 42).
Moreover, the testimony of Wolf-Woman undercut the integrity of what
the Shakhovskiis told the court (see Document 43).

The contradictions of their testimony were highlighted when they
were questioned about Nikolai Kaliuzhnyi, a boy who was supposedly
present when Wolf-Woman told Iuliana Shakhovskaia about the bearded
man who, she claimed, dragged Andrei on the morning of March 12th.
Like their prior testimony, both women offered stories that not only
clashed but also contradicted what they had just told the court. More-

over, Shakhovskaia again insisted that the police instructed her in what to say regarding conversations with Wolf-Woman (see Document 44). Finally, their statements about Kaliuzhnyi were shown to be false when he was sworn in as a witness and questioned by Judge Boldyrev (see Document 45).

Another hole in the prosecution's case concerned the assertions by the Shakhovskiis that Andrei was not carrying any books when they saw him on March 12th. Consequently, the murderer (or murderers) must have placed the books in the cave with the boy's body. It is possible that Andrei had taken the books when he had gone to the brickworks and that Beilis picked up the books after he abducted the boy. But such a supposition depends on Beilis being in fact the murderer. A more likely scenario is that Andrei had left his books at the Cheberiak apartment when he first arrived on the morning of March 12th. Then, after the murder, Vera Cheberiak and the troika decided to hide all evidence that Andrei had visited the apartment by stashing the books with the body. In other words, only the murderers had the motive and opportunity to dispose of the books.

One glaring weakness of the prosecution's case involved Petr Singaevskii, who confessed a year or so after the murder that he and the two other members of the troika and Vera Cheberiak were guilty of killing Andrei. After his dismissal from the force Nikolai Krasovskii persuaded Sergei I. Makhalin, a revolutionary with connections to the criminal underworld, to befriend Singaevskii. Makhalin enlisted the assistance of Amzor E. Karaev, a fellow revolutionary, and the two of them agreed to help Krasovskii because they were outraged by the efforts of the police to frame Beilis. Singaevskii, on his part, was flattered that Karaev, a legendary figure among Kiev's criminals, wanted his help in arranging a prison break. In due time Singaevskii told Karaev and Makhalin about his involvement in the murder of Andrei in order to demonstrate his mettle for criminal activity. At the trial, when Makhalin testified about Singaevskii's admission of guilt, Singaevskii acknowledged that he had met Makhalin, but he denied any involvement in the murder. Even though the government had exiled Karaev to Siberia in order to prevent his taking the stand, the prosecution still managed to pit Singaevskii's word against that of Makhalin when Karaev's statement to Krasovskii, in which he recounted Singaevskii's confession, was read aloud at the trial and entered into the record (see Document 46).

On the stand Vera Cheberiak's testimony did not stand up to the questioning of the defense, and raised suspicions that she was working with the government to affix blame for the murder to Beilis. In mid-1912 she told investigators that before his death Zhenia claimed that Beilis had grabbed both him and Andrei. It never occurred to the police to question why it took her over a year to recall this critical piece of evidence. Most likely she simply made it up on her own or in cahoots with Chaplinskii in order to give the prosecutor what he wanted: additional material that could be used against Beilis, no matter how unlikely and unreliable it was (see Document 47).

The jury also heard evidence suggesting that throughout the investigation Cheberiak worked hard to shift suspicion from herself and the gang to others. For example, at first she accused Andrei's mother and stepfather of the murder. Then, after meeting Brazul'-Brushkovskii, she claimed that her former lover, a young Frenchman named Pavel Miffle, killed Andrei. Moreover, she accused Miffle's sister of poisoning the two Cheberiak children in an act of vengeance after Cheberiak, in late 1910, threw sulfuric acid at Miffle's face in a fit of jealousy. He retaliated by telling the police that she was responsible for a rash of unsolved crimes. Consequently, the police arrested Cheberiak, who spent some of early 1911 behind bars. Testimony presented at the trial, however, showed that she acted vindictively against the Miffles in an effort to throw the investigation off her trail.

In addition, defense lawyers challenged Vasilii Cheberiak's deposition from late 1911 that Beilis had chased Zhenia and Andrei. According to Vasilii, his son immediately reported to him that Beilis and two other men dressed like religious Jews had dragged Andrei toward the kiln. But Oskar Gruzenberg demonstrated in his questioning that Vasilii was at work when Andrei purportedly told him about the events at the brickworks (see Document 48). Furthermore, a neighborhood girl refuted testimony offered by Liudmila Cheberiak, the surviving Cheberiak daughter, that she and other children had witnessed the abduction. The prosecution's assertion that several men had seized Andrei in plain view of a group of children, not to mention employees of the brickworks, is ludicrous. One would expect the children to go running to their parents in the aftermath of such an abduction, but no adult in the neighborhood brought the matter to the attention of the police. In addition, according to the government's account, Beilis, who was busy at work all morning, found the time to take a break, grab and drag Andrei to the kiln, kill the boy, and then return to work without anyone noticing. Moreover, Beilis and his accomplices would have needed to know prior to March 12th that the neighborhood children intended to play at the brick factory in order to ensure the success of the plan. Such a scenario underscores the lack of logic in the prosecution's case.

On the fourth day of the trial Vera Cheberiak pulled a stunt that backfired. Hoping to lend credibility to her testimony that her son had told her that he and the other children had witnessed Beilis grab Andrei, she approached a young boy named Zarutskii, who was waiting in the antechamber of the courtroom before he testified. According to a woman who overheard the conversation and reported it to court officials, Cheberiak asked Zarutskii to lie and say he witnessed Beilis seize Andrei on the morning of March 12th. When the judge summoned both of them to clarify what happened, Zarutskii refused to tell the court the lie proposed by Cheberiak. While it was a case of "he said, she said," and the court let the matter drop, the exchange between Zarutskii and Cheberiak revealed problems with the latter's testimony (see Document 49).

Cheberiak's honesty also came into question when she testified that the journalist Brazul'-Brushkhovskii cajoled her into going to Kharkov in early 1912, where, according to Cheberiak, he promised to introduce her to a member of the State Duma who was in a position to help her. She stated that the member of State Duma was none other than Arnold Margolin, who, it will be recalled, agreed to meet her and Brazul'-Brushkovskii in Kharkov. According to Cheberiak, Margolin offered her, on behalf of wealthy Jews, the hefty sum of 40,000 rubles if she would confess to the murder and assured her he would guarantee that she would never stand trial. Brazul'-Brushkovskii, Margolin, and a detective by the name of Vygranov (who had accompanied the journalist and Cheberiak to Kharkov) all testified that Cheberiak's account of what occurred in Kharkov was pure fiction (see Documents 50 and 51). It was clear to them that Cheberiak had conjured up the story about knowing someone in Kharkov who could shed light on the murder in order to string along Brazul'-Brushkovskii. When it turned out that she would be meeting Margolin, who was a member of the Kiev city council, not the State Duma, Cheberiak decided to embellish her story by making up the tale about Margolin offering her money.

Finally, the testimony of Krasovskii bolstered the defense's claim that Beilis was innocent. On the stand Krasovskii explained why he suspected Vera Cheberiak of involvement in the murder of Andrei, and testified to what the two Diakonova sisters said occurred in the Cheberiak apartment on the morning of March 12th. He also corroborated Adam Polishchuk's testimony (see Document 18) regarding Zhenia Cheberiak's behavior when the police questioned him in August 1911, just before he died. Krasovksii also stated that he believed Andrei had been involved in illegal activities under the direction of Cheberiak, perhaps even helping the gang in a plan to rob the church school he attended. No evidence supports Krasovskii's assertion (see Document 52).

Knowing that they would have difficulty proving Beilis's guilt, the prosecution decided to implicate other unknown Jews in the ritual murder of Andrei. In other words, Beilis would not be the only person on trial: the entire Jewish community and its religion were to be held responsible for the brutal killing of a Christian youth. The prosecution called upon several expert witnesses to provide forensic, psychological, and religious testimony that purportedly showed how Andrei was the victim of a ritual murder committed by Jews following the strictures of Judaism. This supposedly expert testimony, however, was anything but that, revealing that the government was stubbornly going ahead with the case despite the lack of evidence.

The testimony of Father Justin Pranaitis, a disgraced Roman Catholic priest who was one of the few men of the cloth to support publicly the ritual murder accusation, reveals the willingness of the government to countenance any evidence, no matter how fanciful or weak. Most significantly, the prosecution could find only one Russian Orthodox priest or theologian willing to testify.[7] In 1892 Pranaitis had written a pamphlet purportedly proving that Judaism required the ritual sacrifice of gentiles.[8] The pamphlet generated a mild stir among antisemites, but soon after its publication Pranaitis fled to Tashkent because police in St. Petersburg accused him of extorting money from people in the capital. The police allowed him to return to St. Petersburg in 1911 after he agreed to testify on behalf of the government. On the stand Pranaitis argued that the Talmud sanctioned the killing of non-Jews, notwithstanding the Judaic stricture against taking a human life. Moreover, the killing of non-Jews would hasten the arrival of the Messiah and served the important ritual function of blood sacrifice. According to the priest, who drew upon the work of a converted rabbi, Jews allegedly used Christian blood for its supposed magical and medicinal purposes, and at certain religious rites such as weddings, circumcisions, and the baking of matzo. Pranaitis made a fool of himself on the stand, and Beilis's defense team handily ripped to shreds the priest's testimony during cross-examination. Defense attorneys demonstrated the priest's utter ignorance of Judaism and the Talmud, pointing out, among other things, that he had difficulty reading Hebrew. The defense also called to the stand several witnesses, most of whom were non-Jewish theologians, who challenged the priest's translations and interpretations of Judaic texts, and questioned whether he could even read the texts on which he based his assertions. The prosecution responded that it was not necessary to test the ability of Pranaitis to read Hebrew texts, warning the judge that the defense wanted to test the priest's expertise by having him read dozens of books for the court (see Document 53).

The prosecution also elicited the testimony of other so-called experts to support the forensic argument that Andrei's murder was carried out with the intent to drain blood from the body, despite the absence of evidence supporting the prosecution's version of events. The body showed no signs of the intentional cutting of blood vessels to facilitate the collection of blood or evidence that some sort of suction device was used. Moreover, the killer's weapon, most likely an awl, would have difficulty puncturing veins and arteries. Someone intent on maximizing the collection of blood would not have stabbed the victim after he was dead, yet many of the wounds were inflicted after death. Still, the prosecution would not let the autopsies deter their efforts to pin the murder on Beilis.

They found one expert witness in the person of Professor Dmitrii P. Kosorotov of Moscow State University. A specialist in forensic medicine, Kosorotov supported the government's claim that the wounds found on Andrei's body were inflicted for the purpose of obtaining as much blood as possible. But evidence uncovered by the Provisional Government's commission on the case in 1917 showed that the tsarist government paid Kosorotov 4,000 rubles for his testimony, an expense approved by Shcheglovitov himself. Kosorotov claimed that the money was payment for lost earnings and denied that any government official influenced his testimony. Some police officials, however, suggested that the money was a *quid pro quo*.[9]

Another witness for the prosecution was Ivan Sikorskii, the professor of psychiatry who repeated at the trial what he had asserted in 1911 regarding the ritual nature of the murder. During cross-examination by defense lawyers Sikorskii revealed his deep-seated hatred of Jews, voicing timeworn stereotypes of Jews as members of a fanatical religion intent on undermining Christian society and culture. He also mentioned that he offered a course on the "traditional Jewish method" of murdering gentile children. When asked by the court to substantiate his assertions about this "Jewish method" with concrete evidence, he demurred, claiming that regulations on censorship prevented his doing so (see Document 54).

Finally, in order to bolster its assertion that Beilis and unidentified Jews murdered Andrei for religious purposes, the prosecution went to ridiculous lengths to demonstrate that Beilis was a religious zealot and that the Zaitsev brick factory was a hotbed of religious extremism. The government noted that Beilis's father had belonged to a Hasidic sect of Jews. The prosecution, however, conveniently ignored the fact that Beilis himself was not particularly observant and his lifestyle had little if nothing in common with the lives of Hasidim or any religious Jews for that matter. To be sure, Beilis had grown up with knowledge of Judaism, but as an adult he had attenuated ties to religion. He no longer observed Jewish holidays, except for Rosh Hashanah and Yom Kippur, and as we know, he worked on the Sabbath. Indeed, Beilis was at work on March 12th, the day he supposedly committed the murder. No religiously observant Jew, let alone a Hasid, would work on the Sabbath. Despite the defendant's secular lifestyle, the prosecution nevertheless insisted that the defendant had ties to the Hasidim. The government claimed that a certain Feivel Schneersohn, whom Beilis hosted on several occasions, was the scion of the illustrious Hasidic dynasty of the same name. Schneersohn, however, was simply a hay and straw merchant who was not related to his namesake. Indeed, he had never even heard of the Hasidic dynasty when questioned by the police.[10] The prosecution stressed that Jonah Zaitsev, founder of the brick factory, while not a Hasid, was a pious and observant Jew. However, Mark Zaitsev who took over the business when his father died in 1907, rarely attended synagogue and even served non-kosher food to guests. He had also discontinued his father's practice of baking matzo with specially grown wheat under strict rabbinical supervision. In spite of overwhelming evidence to the contrary, the government argued at the trial that Beilis had maintained connections with Hasidism and argued that the Zaitsev family was continuing the supposedly extremist religious behavior of Jonah Zaitsev.[11]

A travesty of justice, the Beilis trial tarnished the tsarist regime's reputation in the court of world opinion. Rather than convince foreign governments that the autocracy's treatment of Jews was justified, the prosecution of Beilis on trumped-up charges embarrassed the regime and highlighted the anachronistic nature of its harsh policies toward Jews. The trial confirmed the view that Tsar Nicholas II's autocratic government was a bastion of antisemitism with nothing but contempt for the rule of law, and led to more, not less scrutiny of the state's discriminatory treatment of Jews.

FOUR

Summation and Verdict

All members of the prosecution gave closing statements in support of the government's claim that Andrei was the victim of a ritual murder in which Beilis participated. As one of the civil plaintiffs seeking damages for Andrei's family, Aleksei Shmakov took an active role in court proceedings. For Shmakov, it was of paramount concern that the jury render a guilty verdict regarding the ritual nature of the murder. A fervent antisemite who relished the opportunity to pepper his questioning of witnesses with mini-lectures about Jewish customs and beliefs drawn from his prodigious reading of obscure pamphlets and books, Shmakov laced his comments with bitter invectives about the evil nature of Jews and Judaism. Earlier in the proceedings Shmakov denied that Vera Cheberiak and her gang killed Andrei, but by the time of his summation, annoyed with revelations regarding Cheberiak's lies and machinations, he offered the unlikely scenario that Cheberiak and Beilis were both guilty of murdering Andrei. According to Shmakov, Cheberiak lured the boy to her apartment and then handed him over to Beilis, who did the actual killing.

The other civil plaintiff, Grigorii Zamyslovskii, devoted much of his summation to bolstering the claim of ritual murder and countering the argument that Cheberiak was involved in the crime. He did not underscore the veracity of those witnesses who based their testimony on what

Zhenia Cheberiak purportedly told them prior to his death; he simply ignored testimony that did not support his version of events. Zamyslovskii also hinted that Vera Cheberiak was afraid of Beilis and the owner of the brick factory because of what they knew about her criminal activities. According to Zamyslovskii's fuzzy logic, Cheberiak's innocence necessarily meant that Beilis was guilty (see Document 55).

The prosecutor Oskar Vipper spoke for five hours when he summarized the case for the jury. He stated that all the defense witnesses had been bribed or frightened by a cabal of Jewish communal leaders. Like Zamyslovskii, Vipper asserted that Cheberiak was innocent, insisting that "international Jewry" had mobilized to secure the acquittal of Beilis at any cost. According to Vipper, it was Jews who raised the issue of ritual murder and blood libel in order to deflect attention away from Beilis and the murder itself. In his remarks he mouthed antisemitic beliefs that Jews dominated gentile society, particularly through their control of the press (see Document 56).

Oskar Gruzenberg, who served as head consul and had defended a Jew of ritual murder charges a decade or so earlier, believed that the trial of Beilis represented the clash of two cultures, one rooted in popular belief, superstition, and ignorance, the other based on reason and knowledge.[1] He stated that it was a mistake to engage the prosecution's argument about the supposed need of Jews for Christian blood. In his mind, an individual Jew, not Judaism, was on trial. Gruzenberg reasoned that it was pointless to dispute a popular belief for which no evidence had ever been presented. As he wrote in his memoirs, "In court there should be only one goal: to prove that the person charged with ritual murder did not commit the murder. It is imperative not to permit even one courtroom verdict convicting a Jew of ritual murder. This is the only thing that is important."[2] Consequently, he devoted most of his remarks to showing the weaknesses of the prosecution's case, particularly the inconsistencies in the testimony of various witnesses with regard to Beilis (see Document 57). Vasilii Maklakov also focused on demonstrating the innocence of the defendant in a stirring and moving summation. He confronted head on the case presented by the prosecution and pointed out all the absurdities in the government's evidence. He maintained that Vera Cheberiak had manufactured the testimony that incriminated Beilis, instructing her husband and daughter to give false testimony against Beilis (see Document 58).

At the end of the summation on the evening of October 28th, Judge Boldyrev charged the jury, which then went into seclusion to deliberate. In his instructions, however, Boldyrev expressed his view that the prosecution had demonstrated to his satisfaction that a ritual murder had occurred on the premises of the brick factory, choosing to overlook the overt weaknesses of the testimonies of the government's witnesses. Clearly aware that the case against Beilis was hopeless, the judge followed the example of the indictment, which had divided the accusations into two parts, and the strategy of the prosecution. The splintering of indictments and charges to the jury was common practice in Russian courts, and allowed jurors to issue mixed verdicts that supported part of the prosecution's case. In the Beilis case, jurors could conclude that a crime as outlined by the prosecution had been committed, but still claim that the defendant was innocent of committing the crime. In other words, splintering allowed the jury to avoid a straightforward guilty or innocent verdict.

The first question posed by Boldyrev focused on whether or not the murder had the characteristics of a ritual murder, while the second concerned the involvement of Beilis and other unknown Jews in the murder. The judge hoped that separating the two charges would help the jury in its deliberations and thereby save the prosecution from losing altogether. The lack of any mention of Judaism and Jews speaks to the government's efforts to shield itself from accusations of antisemitism, notwithstanding the fact that witnesses for the prosecution claimed that Jews and Judaism played a critical role in the murder. Still, his focus on the agonizing death of Andrei and the detailed description of the wounds revealed Boldyrev's attempt to encourage the jury to reach a guilty verdict (see Document 59).

After deliberating for several hours, the jury, early on the morning of October 29th, told the judge that it had reached a decision. On the first count the jury voted seven-to-five that the murder had the hallmarks of a ritual murder and had occurred at the brick factory; on the second the jury was reportedly split evenly, six-to-six, on the issue of Beilis's involvement. One juror reportedly changed his guilty vote to not guilty at the last moment, thereby ensuring a tied vote. Under Russian law a tied vote went in favor of the defendant, and so Beilis was a free man. Despite the lack of physical evidence placing the murder at the brick factory, the government's gamble that the jury would embrace the accusation of ritual murder paid off. And the government demonstrated to the satisfaction of half the jury that Beilis was guilty.[3]

It seemed as if all of Kiev awaited the verdict. Crowds began gathering outside the courthouse once news that the jury was deliberating became known. Police and soldiers heightened their level of preparedness, ready to act in the event of public disturbances. By morning the news of Beilis's acquittal had become the talk of Kiev and quickly circulated to the rest of the Russian Empire and abroad. Many Kievans began to gather outside the Cheberiak apartment in the expectation that the police might continue the investigation there. On October 29th *Kievskaia mysl'* ran the following headline: "Beilis is innocent. There is still justice in Russia. . . . The simple [*serye*] folk have saved the honor of Russia," a reference to the jurors. The paper's editorial the following day noted, "not only was the life of an innocent person saved, but the honor, dignity, culture, and greatness of our homeland were saved."[4] Nevertheless, the fact that seven and six jurors, respectively, found in favor of the government undercuts the faith the newspaper placed in the jury composed of ordinary people and reveals the antisemitism manifest in late Imperial Russian society. Elsewhere in the Russian Empire, Europe, and the United States, newspapers proclaimed that Beilis had been acquitted (see Document 60).

The jury's decision that the killing resembled a ritual murder was significant. Even though Beilis was not held responsible, the government's strategy of demonstrating that a ritual murder had occurred had worked. The tsarist regime presumably welcomed the jury's affirmation of the charge and felt vindicated for spending over two years trying to frame an innocent man. Immediately after the announcement of the verdict, Shmakov made clear that the government's goal had been achieved, namely, that ritual murder posed a genuine threat[5] (see Document 61). In an interview given on October 30th, Zamyslovskii expressed his displeasure with the verdict and stated, "I am convinced that Beilis is guilty." But he added that the government would not appeal because "the main task of the trial was proven," namely, that a ritual murder had taken place. According to Zamyslovskii, reopening the investigation for new evidence in order to reveal the perpetrators of the murder would be "superfluous," an admission that the government was not interested in uncovering the real killer or killers.[6] The decision not to appeal the verdict suggests that

Shcheglovitov wanted to put the trial behind him and did not believe that his staff could assemble evidence that would persuade another jury that Beilis was guilty. Consequently, the killer or killers of Andrei were never brought to justice.

The acquittal of Beilis undoubtedly disappointed those who defended the ritual murder charge and clamored for the conviction of Beilis. But they could find some comfort in the verdict: Beilis may have been acquitted, but the fact that the government came close to convicting him must have been satisfying. After all, the government had demonstrated, from their perspective, the reality of ritual murder. As the October 30th *Dvuglavyi orel* proclaimed, "One Jew Is Acquitted, All Kikes Are Found Guilty" and published an editorial that rehashed what the newspaper had persistently charged (see Document 62). Supporters of the regime reacted as if the prosecution had won a conviction. They held a celebratory banquet with Shcheglovitov and Vipper as the honored guests. And the regime rewarded those who had labored on its behalf with promotions: Boldyrev became chief justice of the Kiev Appeals Court, and Tsar Nicholas II presented him with a gold watch. The government promoted Chaplinskii to the Senate, the highest court in the empire, and Zamyslovskii apparently came away a rich man after the government awarded him 25,000 rubles for his services.

Epilogue

Acquittal meant that Beilis's ordeal had ended. After his release from prison, Beilis wanted nothing more than to return to his family and rebuild his life. But he required hospitalization soon after he arrived home and he had to figure out how to support his family since someone else now occupied his job at the brick factory. In his memoir Beilis recounted the moment of his acquittal, his release from custody, and his return to his family and the world as a free man (see Document 63).

The years spent in prison and the trial had turned him into a public figure whose celebrity had captured the attention of people throughout the Russian Empire, Europe, and the United States. He could not escape the scrutiny of the public and the prying eyes of the press. Nor could he put behind him all that he had endured as a victim of the government's campaign to frame him for murder. Only several weeks after the acquittal six Yiddish theaters in New York staged plays on Beilis and the trial, and similar productions took place elsewhere in North America and Europe.[1] Pathé, a film production company in Paris, released a documentary that the tsarist regime prohibited from being shown in Russia. In addition, a film based on the murder, arrest, and trial of Beilis entitled "The Secrets of Kiev, or the Beilis Trial" appeared right after the trial. The tsarist government prevented its showing, but movie houses in several countries in Europe and the United States ran it.

Despite his celebrated status, Beilis had difficulty figuring out how to earn a living. Lucrative and tempting offers came his way. A wealthy Jewish woman in Paris offered him free housing in a lavish building, and many other well-to-do Jews in Europe and the United States gave assurances that they would provide for him and his family if they should choose to move. But he rejected them: concerns over not knowing French, German, and English and worries about the potential ill effects of the weather in Europe on his frail health combined to discourage his taking advantage of these opportunities. Another proposition was a lecture tour of the United States for $40,000 that he declined because he did not wish to spend twenty weeks in a distant country away from his family.

But threatening letters underscored the danger of remaining in Kiev. A committee of prominent Jews working to smooth his re-entry into private life advised Beilis to move his family somewhere safe. By the end of 1913 Beilis made the difficult decision to emigrate. He and his family left Kiev for Palestine. They settled in Tel Aviv, where his children began attending school. He did not say farewell even to his brother and sister since he was afraid of publicizing his departure for fear that antisemites would interfere. As the excerpt from his memoir reveals, Beilis had serious reservations about leaving Kiev (see Document 64).

The outbreak of World War I in August 1914 made it difficult for Beilis to find work, and the Anglo-Palestine Bank, where he had deposited money that benefactors in Kiev had given him came under the management of a German Jew who did not permit Beilis to draw upon his funds. Promises—some vague, others concrete—made by representatives of wealthy Jews to provide for his financial needs went mostly unfulfilled because the war disrupted the transfer of funds from supporters. In the 1920s Beilis moved his family to the United States, settling in New York City where he worked first as a printer and then as a salesman without much success. He never felt comfortable living in the United States and claimed before his death that he still longed for Palestine. His memoir, *The Story of My Sufferings*, appeared first in serial form in a Yiddish newspaper (1925) and then in English the following year. Beilis died in 1934 at age seventy. Several thousand people attended his funeral at the famed Eldridge Street Synagogue on New York's Lower East Side. He is buried at Mt. Carmel Cemetery in Queens, New York. The following inscription is on his grave, reflecting the belief among many Jews that Beilis's ordeal symbolizes the tribulations of all Jews:

Pay attention to this grave
Here lies a holy person, a chosen man
The people of Kiev made him a victim
And upon all Israel spread the travail
Falsely accused him and his community of taking the blood of a
Christian child as demanded by him and his faith for the festival of Passover
They bound him in chains and lowered him into a pit
Many years he did not see the light of day
On behalf of all Israel he was harshly tortured
Pay tribute to this pure and guiltless soul
Who dwells in the shadow of the Lord in the heights of Heaven
Until those who slumber shall awaken life
Menachem Mendel Ben-Tuvia Beilis
Died on 24 Tammus 5694
May his memory be for an eternal blessing
May his soul be bound in the bond of life eternal

What about the other participants in the Beilis Affair? The advent of communist power in 1917 provided the new leaders of Russia with the opportunity to settle scores with tsarist officials whose behavior they viewed as particularly detrimental to the interests of the Russian people. The Bolsheviks executed Minister of Justice Shcheglovitov. Vipper, chief prosecutor of Beilis, managed to find employment with the communist government, but in 1919 the Bolsheviks arrested him. He died in prison that year. The student Golubev died in battle during World War I, and Father Pranaitis died in early 1917. Communists in Kiev shot Vera Cheberiak in 1918 upon the orders of the Kremlin. We do not know why the new rulers of Russia shot her, but presumably her past caught up with her or, not having changed her ways, she was actively supporting the deposed autocracy.

The Beilis Affair's significance goes beyond the concerns of historians and has relevance to the contemporary world, particularly for our understanding of the persistence of antisemitism in societies around the globe. The grave of Andrei Iushchinskii in Kiev has become a site of pilgrimage for nationalists and antisemites, who view him as a martyr, a victim of a vast Jewish conspiracy to destroy the fabric of Russian and Ukrainian culture and society. In 2006 nationalists built a structure over the grave, erected a wooden Russian Orthodox cross, and placed a piece of granite inscribed with a passage from the bill of indictment describing the nature of the stab wounds. Each year since then, on the anniversary of Andrei's murder, hundreds of people congregate at his grave and commemorate his death as a martyr.

The website *Der Stürmer* pays homage to the Nazi newspaper of the same name published between 1923 and 1945, and includes a section on the Beilis Affair.[2] Similarly, television shows, speeches, and books in parts of Europe and the Arab Middle East sometimes focus on the blood libel as part of their anti-Israel propaganda. As late as the mid-1990s some clerics in Italy agitated for the return of the relics of a victim of a purported sixteenth-century ritual murder to his followers; one church publication in Turin devoted space to articles that urged readers to accept the veracity of ritual murder.[3] As recently as April 2012 a member of the Hungarian parliament dredged up the Tiszaeszlár blood libel from the 1880s, claiming that "we do not know what happened."[4] While these expressions of antisemitism may be the provenance of fringe elements in these societies, the possibility exists that political extremists could use the ritual murder accusation to fuel protests and other actions against Jews. Like the *Protocols of the Elders of Zion*, the infamous forgery and hoax that accuses Jews of engaging in a worldwide conspiracy to dominate the world, the blood libel is alive and well in some parts of the world.[5]

The year 2013 is the centenary of the Beilis trial. The fact that the blood libel still resonates among people in different parts of the world should give us pause to reflect on its lessons for us in the early twenty-first century. The power and authority of the state have grown since the early twentieth century, and governments today possess control that the tsar's ministers could not even imagine. Beilis's ordeal highlights the willingness of governments under siege to adopt desperate measures in the hope of holding onto power, and it reveals the capacity of the state to manipulate popular opinion and political outcomes. The Beilis case demonstrates that literacy and education do not necessarily lead to the disappearance of ethnic, national, racial, and religious stereotypes. Indeed, as events in

Andrei's grave in Kiev, 2011. Photographs by author.

the twentieth century demonstrated, even so-called enlightened societies can fall victim to irrational and unsubstantiated ideas that have devastating consequences for society. The Beilis Affair teaches us about the toxic mix of antisemitism and politics and serves as a cautionary tale about the

danger of ethno-religious hatreds to social and political stability. While there is no guarantee that another Beilis case, no matter how unlikely, will not occur, this book provides a historical perspective that can help societies make informed decisions as citizens.

Documents

Document 1: Papal Edict Condemns
Ritual Murder Accusation

In 1272 Pope Gregory X issued an edict calling upon Christians to reject the charge that Jews engaged in ritual murder. He noted that Judaism prohibits Jews from engaging in human sacrifice and consuming human blood.

Source: Jacob Marcus, *The Jew in the Medieval World: A Source Book.* Cincinnati: Hebrew Union College Press, 1999. P. 171.

Since it happens occasionally that some Christians lose their Christian children, the Jews are accused by their enemies of secretly carrying off and killing these same Christian children and of making sacrifices of the heart and blood of these very children. It happens, too, that the parents of these children or some other Christian enemies of these Jews, secretly hide these very children in order that they may be able to injure these Jews, and in order that they may be able to extort from them a certain amount of money by redeeming them from their straits.

And most falsely do these Christians claim that the Jews have secretly and furtively carried away these children and killed them, and that the Jews offer sacrifice from the heart and blood of these children, since their law in this matter precisely and expressly forbids Jews to sacrifice, eat, or drink the blood, or to eat the flesh of animals having claws. This has been demonstrated many times at our court by Jews converted to the Christian faith: nevertheless very many Jews are often seized and detained unjustly because of this. We decree, therefore, that Christians need not be obeyed against Jews in a case or situation of this type, and we order that Jews seized under such a silly pretext be freed from imprisonment, and that they shall not be arrested henceforth on such a miserable pretext, unless—which we do not believe—they be caught in the commission of the crime. We decree that no Christian shall stir up anything new against them, but that they should be maintained in that status and position in which they were in the time of our predecessors, from antiquity till now.

Document 2: An Eighteenth-Century Pope Refutes the Blood Libel

In 1759 Cardinal Lorenzo Ganganelli (later Pope Clement XIV) submitted a report to Pope Clement XIII regarding allegations of ritual murder in Poland. Ganganelli vehemently denounced the charges, proclaiming that no credible evidence has ever been put forward to support them.

Source: Cecil Roth, ed., *The Ritual Murder Libel and the Jew.* The Woburn Press: London, 1935. Pp. 88–89.

In the information of the Bishop of Lutzk ... we read as follows:

We may understand most plainly how many and how great proofs of cruelty towards Christian blood have been given in this kingdom (i.e. Poland) by the perfidious Jewish nation, not only from histories printed all over the world, but also from the judgments in cases of infanticide pronounced before various diocesan courts and also by the executions on the persons of the unfaithful (it is this which gives just offence) that followed in virtue of them from the year 1400 to the present time.

One gathers from the preface to this report that those prejudices about and against which I have reasoned in my first section (comprising Reflections upon the reports in general) exist in the mind of Mgr. the Bishop of Lutzk, and that the aforesaid report relies on those same principles on which were fabricated the accusations against the Jews of Germany, France, Venice, Padua, Verona, Viterbo and Ancona. Therefore, if the Supreme Pontiffs Gregory IX. and Innocent IV. judged such accusations to be baseless (as I have clearly shown), and if the Jews were declared innocent in the other tribunals of Italy; I cannot see how they can be considered guilty of such a crime in Poland alone, and how, from the year 1400 till the present time (that is to say; for nearly four centuries), they have continued to commit it, at the cost of such suffering both in property and in person.

Then, too, it seems that Mgr. the Bishop of Lutzk has shown himself too prone to believe what cannot be true, since, as has been observed, the Jews did not enter Poland till after 1500; so that, not being there in 1400, they could not commit the supposed crime there. Neither is it credible that, hardly having entered Poland, not as conquerors, but almost as slaves, they would have dared at the very beginning to make themselves more odious than they had been in Spain. Here, had they committed such a crime, they would have been killed and not exiled, in the same manner as the Moors were all slaughtered by order of Ferdinand because they were found guilty of murders, some committed and some designed. The Jews who would not embrace our Holy Faith, on the other hand, were merely exiled by the said Ferdinand. If then in Spain, where they dwelt so long and were so wealthy, the Jews were never accused of such a crime, how can it be credible that when they had scarcely arrived in Poland they at once began the epoch of infanticide and homicide?

I should like Mgr., the Bishop of Lutzk to undeceive himself by perusing the Decretal of Innocent IV, cited by me, which is to be found in Baronius, who continued the work of Raynaldus. There he would be able to see the same accusations which he brings against the Jews, together with their complete exoneration by the esteemed Supreme Pontiff.

It is now a hundred years since the Jews in Poland were first accused of such a crime. There were not wanting, however, persons to undertake their defence, and in order that this might be more powerful, they were proclaimed innocent by holy orators from the pulpits. Here is the authority for this statement. The Very Rev. Father Giovanni Battista de' Marini, General of the Order of Preaching Fathers, moved to pity by the Jews of Poland, who were being harassed by his imputation, wrote on February 9th, 1664, a very urgent letter to Father Alan Chodoruski, Provincial of Poland. In this, he instructed the members of his Order in that Kingdom to preach from the pulpit and persuade the people to dismiss the evil opinion which obsessed them concerning the Jews, whom they believed to be the authors of the crime with which we are dealing:

It has been humbly and sorrowfully shewn to us on the part of the unhappy Jews, who dwell scattered throughout the Kingdom of Poland, that they are malignantly traduced with various calumnies and imputations by the ignorant populace and by certain persons hostile to them through private malice; in particular on the charge that they are accustomed to use the blood of Christians in their rite of the Unleavened Bread. . . . We therefore, moved by righteous pity, earnestly charge your Paternity, through yourself and your Order, to succour this unhappy people against all unjust calumnies. . . . Let the Jews find out in this matter that we desire not their destruction but their salvation. . . .

I, FRIAR LORENZO GANGANELLI, CONSULTOR OF THE HOLY OFFICE.

Document 3: Nineteenth-Century Catholic Newspaper Promotes the Ritual Murder Accusation

Jesuits began publishing La Civiltà Cattolica *(Catholic Civilization) in 1850 as an informal arm of the Vatican. Until the 1960s the Vatican did not distance itself from the antisemitic pronouncements of* La Civiltà Cattolica, *which referred to Judaic texts that purportedly obligate Jews to hate gentiles and engage in ritual murder. The following text is from an article published in 1881 about the alleged ritual murder of a baby boy named Simon.*

Source: http://www.romancatholicism.org.

Florence, the 10th of November, 1881

Rome (Our Correspondence)—The Jew Vitale confirms what the Jew Israel revealed about the bloody Passover rite. He reveals the bloody Passover rites celebrated by him and his uncle Solomon that took place in Monza and Milan. He describes St. Little Simon's dreadful martyrdom and talks about his purpose and motivations. . . .

On the 18th of April, when he was questioned why he needed to obtain the above-mentioned child's blood, he answered that he needed his blood to put it into their unleavened pastries to be eaten at Passover. We cannot avoid stressing that Vitale, like Israel as well, when questioned on the cause of the murder, he did not say he had the aim of insulting the Christian Easter; for his aim was to only celebrate their [own feast]. This is better explained as follows; for when he was asked about the reason why they punctured the child and tore his flesh in such a way—as it was natural to insist upon knowing if there were any other reasons for this behavior—and why it was their custom to consume the blood of Christian children, he answered he had already spoken of it by saying only: "There is no other reason, as far as I know, except for the need we Jews have to get Christian blood in order to properly celebrate our Passover." In order to point this out, he soon added: "It is necessary for Jews to get Christian boys' blood every year in order to put it into their unleavened pastries," repeating what he had already declared, without even mentioning that the reason for it was to insult Christ and Christians. That impious rabbinical rite surely involves that second reason. But it is a subordinate reason, for the main one is to comply with a necessary, lawful rite of celebrating Passover....

Vitale had lived with his uncle for almost three years. During this period, at Passovers, he used to eat some unleavened pastries with blood in them, as said before, according to what his uncle had told him....

Vitale had spent three years of his life in Monza, together with his uncle Solomon, and each of those three years he and his uncle had eaten unleavened pastries flavored with the blood of Monza at Passovers. Thus we can understand how authoritative and worthy of respect many local customs which deal with such Jewish murders are, especially going back to the Middle Ages....

When he was questioned why they had hurt the baby in such a way and why they punctured him like that, he replied they hurt him to have his blood, as he said above, and therefore they punctured him and stretched his arms in Jesus' memory. As far as Vitale knew, it seems clear from his reply that the very first intention for that crime was ... the opportunity ... to renew the memory of Passion in *memoriam Iesu*.

Asked if this renewing Jesus' memory was for good or for bad purpose, he replied that they did it to show that they despised Jesus, the God of the Christians, and said that every year they renew His passion.

When they asked him in what manner they renewed this memory, he answered that the Jews renewed this memory every year by putting some Christian boy's blood in their unleavened bread....

He answered that they used to do this by flavoring their buns with Christian blood. However they were guilty of despising Jesus' memory and His Passion all the same, without expressly thinking about it. Their very purpose was to murder Christian children and take their blood to use in their pastries in honor of their Passover....

Document 4: Soviet Historian Accuses
Tsarist Government of Conspiracy

In 1933 the Soviet historian Aleksandr Tager wrote the first compre-
hensive account of the Beilis Affair. Drawing upon archival documents,
Tager asserted that the prosecution of Beilis was a cynical act of des-
peration by a regime in its death throes. The book appeared in English
translation in 1935.

Source: Alexander Tager, *The Decay of Czarism: The Beiliss Trial.*
Philadelphia: The Jewish Publication Society of America, 1935. Pp. xv
and xix. Spelling has been changed for consistency.

Nevertheless the accusation served their (Russian authorities, ed.)
political purposes and in their fear of the impending revolution they re-
sorted to it. Opportunity presented itself in the discovery of the body of
a Christian boy who had been murdered in Kiev and thrown into a cave.

Although the investigations of the police led to a well known band
of criminals, the authorities closed their eyes, shielded the real culprits
and indicted and tried an innocent Jew with the deliberate purpose of
discrediting the Jewish people and their religion in order to cast aspersion
upon the liberal movement and perpetuate the autocratic and corrupt
government of the Tsar....

The indictment, the gathering of the evidence, the expert testimony, the selection of the jury, the appointment of the trial judge and
the prosecuting attorney, and the conduct of the trial itself—all these
were planned and carried out with the most amazing cynicism and in-
sincerity that can only be characterized as monstrous. Those concerned
on the government's side used all manner of evasion and fraud to conceal
the truth and establish a lie to fasten the charge of cruel murder on an
innocent and harmless Jewish workman. The whole plot was nothing
short of diabolical. The officials of the government, from the lowest to
the highest, were in the plot, and the Tsar himself was not unaware of
what was going on....

National chauvinism is the inevitable satellite of the political reaction of our most recent era.... In essence, however, it is always the same:
it is reactionary nationalism, which in its blindness ascribes a privileged
position to one nationality as against other nationalities, looked upon as

inferior. The more consistent, deep and impulsive the reaction in general, the less reserved and more boisterous becomes the nationalist intolerance....

National intolerance was brought to the greatest height in the political regime of the Tsaristic reaction; it was an absolutely official part of governmental policy. All national minorities were oppressed in one form or another: Poles like Finn, Jews like Armenians. The Jews, however, were persecuted in special ways, and much more than the others. Anti-Semitism is the phenomenon *par excellence* in which the national intolerance of reactionary governments and parties expresses itself in the acutest form.

Document 5: American Historian Condemns the Tsarist Government

In 1966 Maurice Samuel, who was attending university in England at the time of the trial, seconded Tager's assessment of the tsarist regime's motives in framing Beilis.

Source: Maurice Samuel, *Blood Accusation: The Strange History of the Beilis Case*. New York: Knopf, 1966. Pp. 4–7. Spelling has been changed for consistency.

What shocked and frightened us in the Beilis case was its sponsorship by a national government. True, this was Russia, the land of absolutism and reaction; but Russia was in, if not wholly, of the twentieth century. She had her ambassadors and consuls in every civilized country; she had her alliances and trade agreements. She must, we thought, have some "decent respect to the opinions of mankind." Her official anti-Semitism was disgraceful enough; and there were the pogroms, for which the government disclaimed responsibility, however unconvincingly. But this! This endorsement in high places of a bugaboo, a blood-stained superstition which had to be defended by Russia's representatives at the Western courts! What did it mean? ...

... the Beilis case was manufactured by Russian governmental authorities expressly to inflame the populace against the Jews....

We could only conclude that it was trying to synthesize two types of anti-Semitism, the modern secularist and the medieval demonological, making a simultaneous play for the "sophisticated" urbanite and the superstitious peasant.

However, the Dreyfus case and the Beilis case had the same fundamental purpose—to arrest and turn back the forces of progress; and time showed that in each instance the particular case was but an episode or an instrument in the larger historical struggle. . . . In Russia the Beilis case was mounted by men who hoped by means of it to strengthen the autocracy and to crush the liberal spirit that was reviving after the defeat of the 1905 revolution. . . .

Document 6: American Historian
Disputes Tsarist Conspiracy

In the 1960s Hans Rogger initiated the scholarly reassessment of the trial. He disputed the existence of a grand conspiracy that originated among Tsar Nicholas II's closest advisers and argued that the plot to frame Beilis began in Kiev and then won the approval of several key ministers.

Source: Hans Rogger, "The Beilis Case: Anti-Semitism and Politics in the Reign of Nicholas II." *Slavic Review*. Vol. 25, No. 4 (December 1966): 616, 622, 624–626, and 629. Permission granted by the Association for Slavic, East European, and Eurasian Studies.

There is no denying that there had been official encouragement or toleration of nationalistic or anti-Semitic excesses on more than one occasion, but the government did not feel sufficiently desperate in the spring of 1911 to make the manufacture of such a case a matter of high policy and an important part of its defense against the revolution. A decision to let the charge of ritual murder be aired in open court had ultimately to be made at the highest level of the administration. That, however, is not where it originated, but in Kiev itself, among members of a local right-wing organization. . . . Nor was the revolutionary wave yet threatening to engulf the old regime when the ritual accusation was first voiced in March and April or when Beilis was arrested in July 1911. . . .

To insist that the Ministers of Justice, Interior and Foreign Affairs as well as the emperor himself knew that it was not Beilis who had killed the boy Andrei is only to compound the difficulty, not resolve it. In the case of Nicholas II, at least, there is every possible indication that the emperor, whose obdurate resistance to political pressures and realities was well-known, believed in the existence of ritual murder and every certainty that he was convinced of the viciousness of the Jews. Learning the jury's verdict, the tsar told a member of his entourage, "It is certain that there was a ritual murder. But I am happy that Beilis has been acquitted, for he is innocent." . . .

A man who took seriously the myth of the Jewish world conspiracy, who asked his police to investigate the links between Jewish Freemasonry and the revolutionaries, who refused to condemn pogroms or to express sympathy for the sufferers—such a man was not influenced, pressured or argued on grounds of political utility into countenancing a ritual murder trial. He did not need to be.

Shcheglovitov was a more complicated man, and it is wrong to ascribe his actions to simple careerism. A desire to please the tsar may have played its part, but not a dominant one, for Nicholas's interest in the matter was both limited and passive, expressed only in response to what the Minister felt his monarch should or would like to know. The Beilis case did not become the Beilis Affair—with the government's prestige staked on its outcome—for almost a year, and there is no reason to think that Nicholas would have pressed for its prosecution on its own. The initiative was Shcheglovitov's. Did he then believe in the reality of the blood sacrifice practiced by the Jews? And did he wish to have this reality established by a court of law for all the world to see although he knew that in this particular instance there had been no ritual murder? The possibility exists, but evidence to make it more than a possibility does not. . . .

If, as is almost certain, Shcheglovitov knew that there was no such thing as ritual murder, his unwavering commitment to the Beilis case and to the men who had inspired it was yet a matter of principle. Or, rather, it was the search for a principle, for a common belief which would rally and bind together the disheartened forces of unthinking monarchism. Unlike liberals and socialists, they had little hope for the future, no confident, comprehensive view of the world and of history that promised success to their cause. Lacking a monarch who could have embodied the autocratic principle with vigor and infectious conviction, they had only anti-Semitism and the notion of universal evil, with the Jews as its carriers, to make sense of a world that was escaping their control and their intellectual grasp. To give visible proof that ritual murder had been committed would confirm such a version of events, give it body and reality. . . .

Such an interpretation of the affair is, admittedly, speculative, particularly where unconscious motivations must have played a larger than usual role, but that is precisely why no purely rational explanation seems to make "sense." . . . There are, however, enough clues in the record to lend substance to a view which takes the affair (and the Judeophobia it reflected) to have been as much a matter of "ideology," of the need for a coherent outlook on the political and social forces at work in the world, as of practical, short-run politics. . . .

There had been no grand design; there had not even been a tactical plan. There had been an experiment, conducted by a small band of unsuccessful politicians and honest maniacs to see how far they could go in imposing their cynicism and their madness on the state. They had succeeded beyond all expectation; they found willing allies in two powerful ministers, the approval of the emperor and the silent acquiescence of other members of the government.

1. THE INITIAL INVESTIGATION

Document 7: Coroner's Report

The psychologist Vladimir Bekhterev published excerpts from the original coroner's report.

Source: V. M. Bekhterev, "The Iushchinskii Murder and the Expert Psychiatric-Psychological Opinion." Translated by Lydia Razran Stone. *Journal of Russian and East European Psychology.* Vol. 41, no. 2 (2003): 24–28. English translation copyright © 2003 by M. E. Sharpe, Inc. Reprinted with permission.

The hands have been tied behind the back with twine, 2 mm thick, in the following manner: the twine had been wrapped around the right wrist and tied in a knot, then tied to the left wrist by crossing the twine that had then been wrapped twice around the joined hands and fastened with a knot on the left . . . The body is of weak build and not well nourished. *Rigor mortis* has passed off and there is virtually none of the subcutaneous blood spots characteristic of cadavers. The hair on the head is blonde, . . .

The eyelids are covered with dried clay. The ears and nose are intact, the external ear canal, nostrils, and lips are covered with dried clay....

Injuries. Shaving the hair on the head to the scalp, and cleaning the scalp and clotted blood, reveals four linear 3–7 millimeter long wounds in the middle part of the crown and a 4 millimeter wound of the same shape on the skin of the left temple. The right temple is covered with fourteen punctate stab wounds. These punctures are scattered on the outer edge of the temple, but are arranged in straight rows on the inner edge. The three punctures in one row are separated by regular .5 centimeter intervals. There are four linear wounds on the right side of the neck, toward the nodding muscles, each about .5 centimeter long, and another similar wound under the left side of the lower jaw. There are two more in the area of the Adam's apple and two stab wounds on the left cheek.

On the left side of the chest between the nipples and hypochondrium (area below the ribs), there are seven stab wounds, . . . There are eight stab wounds in the central area of the xiphoid process. There are five stab wounds on the right side along the axillary line, . . . There are four stab wounds on the right side of the back, along the shoulder blade line....

Chest cavity. The surface of the costal pleura (membrane lining the chest wall) on the left side of the chest cage exhibits six wounds, corresponding to the wounds on the skin described above.... In the anterior part of the pericardium (the membranous sack surrounding the heart) are four punctate wounds, . . . There are four wounds on the surface of the heart around the apex. A probe inserted in one of these could readily be made to exit through the other. A fifth wound is located in the center of the left ventricle, and a sixth in the center of the right ventricle.

Document 8: Call to Arms

The newspaper Evreiskie izvestiia (*Jewish News*) *published the leaflet distributed by Nikolai Pavlovich at Andrei's funeral. As a member of the Union of the Russian People and the Society of the Double-Headed Eagle, Pavlovich hoped to spark retaliation against Kievan Jews.*

Source: *Evreiskie izvestiia* (Jewish News), no. 6 (80) (May 31, 1911): 3.

Orthodox Christians! The kikes have tortured the boy Andrei Iushchinskii.

Every year before their Passover the kikes torture several dozen Christian boys in order to pour their blood into matzo.

The kikes do this to commemorate the suffering of the Savior, whom the kikes tormented and crucified on the Cross.

The coroners found that A. Iushchinskii was bound, undressed and stabbed while he was naked since it was known that stabbing the main veins would extract more blood. The kikes pierced Iushchinskii fifty times.

Russian people! If your children are dear to you, then beat up the kikes! Beat them up so long as one kike lives in Russia! Take pity on your children. Avenge the unfortunate martyr. It's time; it's time!

Document 9: The Black Hundred Press and Ritual Murder

An editorial in the monarchist newspaper Zemshchina *(The Realm) accused the Jewish community of hindering the investigation in the hope of stirring up public opinion against the Jews and winning public sympathy.*

Source: *Zemshchina* (The Realm), no. 624 (April 23, 1911): 2.

Why is it that, when puzzling murders of children are committed in which all the blood is extracted as a result of dozens of wounds, Jews are not busy looking for a solution but only howl in one voice—it's a lie, it's a denunciation, it stirs one part of the population against another . . . ? Why don't Jews try to find out who needs the blood of our youth? . . .

Hearing similar stories about ritual murder obviously confirms the many rumors about Jews. The Russian people are trying to conceal these very evil deeds. And the Jews dare to reproach us for our superstitions? Because . . . an enormous part of society believes in the dark forces out of fear, they rush to announce that they don't believe in ritual murder.

There is nothing at all to believe or not believe. It is necessary only to know the facts and to be among the leaders in history. . . .

Document 10: Jews Accused of Concealing the Truth about the Murder

Zemshchina *(The Realm) published the following article that condemned Jews for their self-serving efforts to prevent the public from learning the truth about ritual murder and Andrei's death.*

Source: *Zemshchina* (The Realm), no. 627 (April 26, 1911): 1.

"Judaic Woe"

Moderate your appetite, Mr. Oppressed, and do not demand that the Russian people once and for all shut their mouths. Surely we do not yet live in a kike republic, but a Russian monarchy. And if you kikes dare to torture our children, then at least reserve us the right to demand the gallows for you. You howl in vain about the incitement of one part of the populace against the other. We are not stirring up the Russian populace against you and demanding retribution, but you are inciting us with your villainous acts, especially when this villainy remains unpunished.

Document 11: Ritual Murder
Described in Detail

The Dvuglavyi orel (*The Double-Headed Eagle*) *offered an account purporting to describe a ritual murder. Reprinted from* Russkoe znamia (*The Russian Banner*)*, the article was an effort to fan the flames of public sentiment against Jews.*

Source: *Dvuglavyi orel* (The Double-Headed Eagle), no. 17 (April 24, 1911): 1.

No, there is no doubt whatsoever that we have here a case of ritual murder carried out by the kikes. According to Judaic law the murder has to be carried out without fail before their Passover holiday with the aim of obtaining blood needed for various rituals. The murder victim . . . must be a Christian who is no older than 13. According to a special rite, five people participate in the murder. The victim is subject to cruel torture: they pierce the body in various places because all victims of ritual murders are always stabbed all over. Previously the kikes crucified one of their own as the victim, but later on they recognized that it was not compulsory and only in the memoirs of those who once engaged in the crucifixions do we learn that they hammered nails into various parts of the condemned.

The blood is drawn out without fail during the torture and while the victim is alive. During the torture and extraction of the blood the victim must be naked and in a standing position. . . . The arms of the victim are bound firmly and the mouth is held shut so the tortured person cannot scream. When the extraction of the blood is over, then the victim is finally killed by stabs to the heart. . . .

We must ring all the bells, sound the tocsin and scream on all the street corners that wild beasts in the form of kike-cannibals will not be tolerated by the Russian state and that the government is committed once and for all to limit this unparalleled fanaticism so that the Orthodox Russian people everywhere do not do so themselves.

Document 12: Editor of Antisemitic Newspaper Appeals for Calm

Despite the strident stance taken by his newspaper regarding the blood libel, the editor of the Dvuglavyi orel *(The Double-Headed Eagle) urged the public not to take matters into its own hands, evidently aware that the authorities would not approve of violent demonstrations against Jews.*

Source: *Dvuglavyi orel* (The Double-Headed Eagle), no. 17 (April 24, 1911): 1.

For over two weeks all the press in the capital and provinces have been heatedly discussing the events in Kiev, namely the murder of Andrei Iushchinskii, a student at the Kiev-Sofia Ecclesiastical Academy and accusing the Jewish sect—the Hasidim—of the murder. The aforementioned press has abundantly stirred understandable alarm among Kievans, the more so since the local press has almost completely remained silent about this incident—biding its time for the end of this affair with the seizure of the real killers. What can we do if the silence is understood by many Kievans and interpreted as an effort by our local administration to paint over this incident? Such an incorrect interpretation is unfortunately supported by educated people who have influence over simple people and have stirred up among the latter still more alarm. They say, do not believe the police, do not believe the judicial powers since all of them have been bribed by the Jews. Hence do not listen and do not stand on ceremony with them. The invitation to disobey the authorities is the same as a call for a rebellion against the government, the same government that our Imperial Majesty has instructed to ensure order in our Fatherland and that we, as monarchists and faithful servants of the Tsar, should not only obey, but support in every way possible. Do you recall the kind of rulers at the time of Jesus Christ? The evil Pilate, the cunning Herod and genuine unbeliever Caiaphus. And what happened? Our savior and his apostles did not rise up in rebellion and insurrection . . . on the contrary they obeyed the leaders' decrees and undertook to follow the example of our Father Jesus Christ.

Furthermore, gentlemen, have faith in the representatives of tsarist power, faith in their impartiality, faith in their sincere desire to serve the tsar and the fatherland. It is only with this faith and trust that you will be able to help find the real murderers who tortured . . . Andriusha Iushchinskii. Excessive ardor has always and can only spoil things. We must calmly wait for the end of the investigation of this outrageous murder.

Document 13: Criticism of the Investigation

In late April 1911 State Duma deputy Grigorii G. Zamyslovskii accused the government of failing to treat Andrei's death as a ritual murder. Zamyslovskii would help the prosecution at the trial.

Source: *Novoe vremia* (New Times), no. 12617 (April 29, 1911): 1.

However, in spite of the fact that Jews, prompted by religious fanaticism, drain the blood from Christian youths, it has been established without a doubt that the government stubbornly refuses to take measures to discover those Jewish sects that adhere to such vile and barbaric rites.

Every time when a murder or an attempted murder as a consequence of such a rite comes to light, the government confines its investigation only to the matter of the specific murder, shutting its eyes to the criminal association and religious learning that push its fellow members toward crime. . . . Instead of taking measures to find out about the fanatical Judaic sect whose members commit murder, the investigation is wasting time by suspecting that Iushchinskii's mother tortured her son. . . .

We present the following questions to the Ministers of Internal Affairs and Justice:

1. Whether it is known to them that in Russia a criminal sect of Jews uses Christian blood for several of their religious rites and whether the members of such a sect tormented the boy Iushchinskii in March 1911 in Kiev as the newspapers reported?

2. If it is known, then what measures are being taken for bringing to the end the existence of this sect and the activities of its members? In addition, what is being done to discover which of its members participated in the torture and murder of the young Iushchinskii?

Document 14: The Existence of Ritual Murder

A founder of the Union of the Russian People, Vladimir M. Purishkevich used the State Duma as a rostrum from which he attacked those he believed were undermining the autocracy, namely Jews and socialists. Andrei's murder afforded him another opportunity to attack Jews verbally and offer his views on ritual murder.

Source: *Novoe vremia* (New Times), no. 12618 (April 30, 1911): 1.

We hope that what the representative of the government has said here is not empty words and that it will take all measures to clarify the nature of the murder, which apparently stems from ritual causes. The monarchist parties are frequently accused of having members who are pogromists. Meanwhile, you know that there has not been one pogrom since the establishment of the first monarchist party. We do not fight with our fists, but with the means of cultural influence. If the murder of the boy Iushchinskii is obscured, if the truth is not elucidated, then you yourself are to blame. I say this with the full knowledge of the people's soul . . . since I myself come from the midst of the people.

If there are no Jewish sects that advocate ritual murder, then it is important to the Jews themselves that the truth triumphs. In interviews the representative of the Jewish people, Deputy Nesselrode[1] has said that perhaps such fanatics exist among Jews (Nesselrode shouts, "Not true.").

But if such fanatics do exist, then why don't the Jews themselves fight them . . . ? The existence of ritual murder is supported by documentation that cannot be disputed. In 1710 a converted Jewish rabbi, Serafimovich, in Lvov solemnly revealed Jewish secrets about child killing and acknowledged that he had carried out such murders several times. He indicated that every Jewish boy and girl at the age of 13 contributed two *złotys* every year for the purchase of victims. This money is entrusted to a Jew known for his modesty and steadfastness. This Jewish agent takes up residence in some town and catches a Christian child. The Jews imprison the child in a ... cellar and feed him various tasty tidbits: almonds, raisins, and milk. They treat the child affectionately without any sign that they are expecting a sacrifice. When the fatal day comes, a rabbi and a selected group of pious Hasidic Jews enter the cellar. The rabbi caresses the child and suddenly stabs him with a little knife from a golden case that is specially kept for this rite. The Jews suggest that if they begin the sacrifice in this manner the blood of the children will not spoil. Then they tie, and sometimes nail, the child to a cross, and the rabbi stabs him with the knife on the right side of the body and places a basin under the body for the flowing blood. While doing this, the rabbi utters the following words:

"Just as we tortured the Christian God, who gave his name to children, so must we torture a Christian child."

From the audience: "Crazy fairy tale."

Purishkevich: After this they place the child in a barrel with nails protruding into its interior. They roll the barrel with such precision so that the nails do not touch either the heart or head. Then they pull out the child from the barrel and kill him. They throw the body of the child in manure or water or they burn the body. But they do not bury it. The Talmud forbids the burial of the dying. ... This is the story shared by Rabbi Serafimovich. Perhaps at the present time they manage to do so without nails and barrels, but a fact remains a fact. You must refute our claims not with shouts, but with documents.

1. Count Anatolii D. Nesselrode, political liberal and grandson of Karl Nesselrode, foreign minister under Tsar Alexander I.

Document 15: The Government Response

An official from the ministry of justice took issue with the accusations lodged by Zamyslovskii and Purishkevich and stressed that the ritual murder accusation is an unproven rumor.

Source: *Kievlianin* (The Kievan), no. 119 (May 1, 1911): 2–3.

As we know, the question about ritual murders, that is, about murders committed out of religious fanaticism, is very old and extremely controversial. In the first century the Romans accused Christians of these murders, and then in the Middle Ages similar accusations against Jews arose and called forth a series of trials that have been repeated until our time in various countries including Russia. Although courts in the Middle Ages and in much later epochs issued several guilty verdicts, all these trials were so darkened by ignorance that they did not prove the existence of special fanatical sects that engage in ritual murder. The question still remains extremely controversial. When the supposition about the possibility of ritual murder is unproven, then it remains in the realm of legend and conjecture. It is impermissible to call any mysterious murder a ritual murder when all we can say is that we do not know anything about it. Almost every mysterious (*temnoe*) crime can give rise to dozens of guesses, dozens of suggested explanations, but all of them do not have the slightest value since they are built either on fantasy or lack the basis of its conclusions.

We declare that the malicious gossip and slanderous reproaches thrown from the rostrum of the Duma were introduced by the authors of the interpellation for the sake of arousing the Christian population against the Jews and instigating a pogrom. Recognizing that the hypothesis about ritual murders is unproven, we however understand that not a small number of people absolutely and sincerely believe in the existence of such a horrible acts . . . and absolutely and sincerely are worried. But the members of the State Duma occupy a position of responsibility that obligates them not to lend credence to ignorant rumors, guesses, and unverified idle talk and gossip.

Document 16: A Bastion of Monarchism Breaks Ranks

For nearly fifty years Kievlianin (The Kievan) had been a mouthpiece for conservative politics. But the editor and publisher of the newspaper rejected the illogic of the right wing's insistence that Andrei had been the victim of ritual murder.

Source: *Kievlianin* (The Kievan), no. 119 (May 1, 1911): 2.

The question about ritual murders is very old and extremely controversial. Christians in the first centuries were accused of these murders by the Romans. By the Middle Ages the accusation against the Jews had already arisen, which led to a series of trials. Even though the trials of the Middle Ages as well as those that came later led to several guilty sentences, all these trials nevertheless ... did not prove the existence of a sect that engaged in ritual murder. When the suggestion about ritual murder is not proven, when it remains in the realm of legend and conjecture, then ... ritual murder is ... a mysterious crime about which we can only say that we do not know anything. If almost every obscure crime can only elicit dozens of conjectures and dozens of supposed explanations, then they all lack any value since they are built either on fantasy or lack logical explanations.

Document 17: The Police Interview Zhenia Cheberiak

Vera Cheberiak's behavior when police investigators interviewed her son Zhenia in August 1911 reinforced the belief of some police officials that she was involved in Andrei's murder and was trying to prevent knowledge of her involvement from becoming public. At the trial Evtikhii Kirichenko, a police captain, offered testimony supporting the view that Vera Cheberiak was in some manner involved in the murder.

Source: *Delo Beilisa: Stenograficheskii otchet.* Volume 2. Kiev, 1913. P. 41.

At the time of the search I found myself in the same room as Cheberiak's boy. A police officer was in the living room, and ... I had a conversation with Zhenia Cheberiak and asked him about the murder of the Iushchinskii boy. He wanted to tell me something, but suddenly he paused and said that he didn't remember. I was sitting on one side of the door, and he was on the other. Cheberiak herself was in the adjacent room ... and observed our conversation. When I asked Zhenia who killed Iushchinskii I noticed that his face twitched. I somehow instinctively looked at the adjacent room and ... saw that Cheberiak ... was making a threatening gesture with her hand. Along with Zhenia I understood this gesture. This gesture made such a strong impression upon me that I began to worry. I ended the search, left the apartment, ... It was my assumption that ... Cheberiak undoubtedly was involved in the murder. Otherwise, why would she make such a threatening gesture if she were not mixed up in the murder?

Document 18: Vera Cheberiak Asks Her Son
to Maintain Her Innocence

Shortly before her son Zhenia's death in August 1911, Vera Cheberiak pleaded with him to tell the police investigators that she had nothing to do with Andrei's murder. In the following exchange at the trial the detective Adam Polishchuk responded to questions posed by Aleksei S. Shmakov, an attorney working on behalf of Andrei's mother.

Source: *Delo Beilisa: Stenograficheskii otchet.* Volume 1. Kiev, 1913.
Pp. 283–85.

SHMAKOV: Were you present at the times when Zhenia became conscious? What did Vera Cheberiak say?

POLISHCHUK: "Tell me who the real murderer is."

SHMAKOV: Did she say: "Tell me, dear son, so they don't disturb me?"

POLISHCHUK: She said, "Tell them who is the murderer so they leave me alone."

SHMAKOV: And how did he respond?

POLISHCHUK: He didn't respond.

SHMAKOV: Didn't he say, "Leave me alone, mama, it is hard for me to remember."

POLISHCHUK: It is possible, but I don't remember just now. . . .

OSKAR O. GRUZENBERG (head of Beilis's defense team): When the boy came to consciousness, what did his mother say to him when you questioned him?

POLISHCHUK: She would not let him speak.

GRUZENBERG: She didn't let him speak?

POLISHCHUK: That's right.

GRUZENBERG: How do you explain the fact that the mother interfered with his answering your questions?

POLISHCHUK: That it was difficult for him to speak and the mother didn't want us to trouble him.

GRUZENBERG: But didn't she say to the boy, "Tell them, dear little son, that your mama had nothing to do with the murder."?

POLISHCHUK: She said that. . . .

GRUZENBERG: What did the child say to his mother's request?

POLISHCHUK: The boy did not answer. . . .

GRUZENBERG: When you were questioned not about this matter but the deaths of the children, didn't you say that the boy said, "Leave me in peace, mother?"

POLISHCHUK: I don't remember.

Document 19: Nikolai Krasovskii Complains about Interference in His Investigation

Nikolai A. Krasovskii was the initial lead investigator of Andrei's murder, and by the summer of 1911 his suspicions fell on Vera Cheberiak. However, the officials intent on railroading Beilis managed to have Krasovskii removed from the case, replacing him with someone who was more pliable and compliant.

Source: *Delo Beilisa: Stenograficheskii otchet.* Volume 1. Kiev, 1913. Pp. 538 and 541.

In my opinion the case was the work of a gang of thieves. . . . I frequently encountered . . . Golubev and others, all of whom were extremely interested in the case. At that time rumors were circulating that the murder was committed by Jews for a ritual purpose. The above-named persons, who were members of a monarchist organization, were very interested in the case. When I was engaged in my investigation, they very frequently asked my opinion of the case. At the same time the press raised a big stink whenever one of my actions did not satisfy these monarchist organizations. . . . I immediately reported to the prosecutor that measures needed to be taken so they did not interfere with the course of the investigation and did not have an effect on those persons who would be interrogated. . . .

Document 20: Vera Cheberiak's Neighbor Testifies about Suspicious Sounds on the Day of the Murder

Zinaida Malitskaia lived in the apartment below Vera Cheberiak, where she ran a wine store attached to the apartment. Her testimony supported the scenario that Andrei was murdered in Cheberiak's apartment.

Source: *Delo Beilisa: Stenograficheskii otchet.* Volume 2. Kiev, 1913. Pp. 27–28.

JUDGE FYODOR A. BOLDYREV: Witness, please tell us what you know about this case.

MALITSKAIA: I don't know anything about the Beilis case.

BOLDYREV: What do you know about the murder of Iushchinskii?

MALITSKAIA: I know what I heard—that's a fact. I heard a suspicious sound, a fuss of some sort, the steps of a child, something out of the ordinary. Whether she was killing Iushchinskii or someone else, I cannot say. But I did hear something—that's a fact. I can tell more about this in detail.

BOLDYREV: Can you tell us the details?

MALITSKAIA: It was like this: at the beginning of March 1911, when my husband was away for a long time, I heard a child's footstep in the Cheberiaks' apartment.

BOLDYREV: Where did you hear the steps?

MALITSKAIA: The footsteps went from one room to another. The steps went from the small corridor to the main room. Then I heard a door being slammed and then a child's scream and weeping. . . . I heard the steps of adults going . . . toward the source of the scream and weeping. I heard a sound, . . . a whisper, and then the muffled sound of a child. At that point I had to tear myself away to take care of customers. . . . I heard steps—the steps of adults were especially clear, but already the steps of the child were not so audible. It was as if two people were dancing . . . back and forth. Then I heard other steps. I heard nothing more except for whispering. It occurred to me that this was not the child of Cheberiak. Zhenia wore boots and walked like an adult. . . . I didn't realize at the time that the voices were of other children, not those of Cheberiak. When I returned to the store a woman told me that she had met Cheberiak's children on the street. That's all I know. . . .

OSKAR VIPPER (state prosecutor): You said that children's steps could be heard and you decided that they were not Zhenia's since Zhenia walked in boots like an adult. Did you hear the footsteps clearly?

MALITSKAIA: I heard clearly.

VIPPER: And you could distinguish which steps were Zhenia's, which were Valia's, and which were Liuda's?

MALITSKAIA: I could distinguish who was walking in boots and who was walking in shoes.

VIPPER: And you could clearly tell who was talking in a high voice and who in a low voice?

MALITSKAIA: Yes, I could.

VIPPER: And consequently you could tell in which room Cheberiak or her children were talking?

MALITSKAIA: Yes. If they said "mmh," I heard "mmh." If Cheberiak said "mmh," I also heard "mmh." (Laughter in the courtroom)

BOLDYREV: I ask you not to laugh.

ZAMYSLOVSKII: What time was it?

MALITSKAIA: I cannot say exactly . . . somewhere between ten and eleven.

ZAMYSLOVSKII: Please be more specific as to what then happened. I would like to know in detail if there were steps, a shout, and a whine.

MALITSKAIA: I cannot describe it in more detail because I was so busy, constantly running between the store and the room. There was a commotion and they were carrying something. . . . I heard them carrying something unwieldy. . . . Then I heard steps going to the other room as if they were dragging something. As if they were carrying something and putting it on the floor. If they put something hard on the floor, then I would have heard it. . . . I now understand what they were carrying and who had screamed. . . .

GRUZENBERG: When you talked to your husband . . . about the incident, did he not say that you should go to the authorities, that it was wrong to conceal such things?

MALITSKAIA: He said to me that it was the duty of all honest persons to report the incident even though there might be consequences.

GRUZENBERG: And he insisted that you go and tell the authorities?

MALITSKAIA: Yes, without fail. . . .

ALEKSANDR S. ZARUDNYI (defense attorney): You said that your husband impressed upon you to talk to the authorities, that this is the duty of any honest person, even if you would suffer as a consequence. What did you understand by this word? How is it possible to suffer if you tell the truth?

MALITSKAIA: Cheberiak threatened to burn my eyes because I imprudently asked her "what happened" after I heard the noise.

Document 21: Additional Testimony Casts Suspicion on Vera Cheberiak

Vera Cheberiak invited her friend Ekaterina Diakonova to spend a night after Andrei's disappearance. In her testimony Diakonova suggested that the boy's corpse was in the apartment a few days after he went missing.

Source: *Delo Beilisa: Stenograficheskii otchet.* Volume 1. Kiev, 1913. Pp. 607–609.

JUDGE BOLDYREV: Tell us what you saw when you spent the night there. . . . Tell us everything.

EKATERINA DIAKONOVA: She came to me and asked me to spend the night.

BOLDYREV: When was this?

DIAKONOVA: It was the evening of March 13. It seems to me that it was the 13th.

BOLDYREV: It's very important to know if you can recall whether it was the 13th or 14th.

DIAKONOVA: I didn't spend the night of the 13th there. . . . At first Cheberiak came to me and asked me to spend the night. That was the 13th. Cherniakova[1] and I went over, but then we became frightened. We became frightened and so we left and didn't spend the night. Cheberiak shut the door, left a lamp burning in the apartment, and all three of us left. Cherniakova went home, and Cheberiak and I went to my apartment. Then the next day she again asked me to spend the night. I agreed and went over and slept in the small room. . . .

BOLDYREV: Did you undress to sleep?

DIAKONOVA: I slept with my boots on, but I don't recall if I was dressed or not. My boots bothered me and so I woke up and took them off. While I was asleep it seemed to me that someone was standing nearby. I woke up. Cheberiak said to me, "Why did you wake up? Go to sleep?" I said to her, "It seemed to me that someone was standing here." She again said, "Go to sleep." I don't know who was standing there, but there was something near the wardrobe. I don't know what, but when I stretched my legs it seemed to me that something was standing there. Cheberiak again told me not to pay attention to it.... I fell asleep. In the morning she woke me and told me to have some tea....

VIPPER: She had only one bed?

DIAKONOVA: Yes, one bed.

VIPPER: So you shared the bed?

DIAKONOVA: Yes....

VIPPER: You lie in bed and hit something solid with your foot? What did you hit?

DIAKONOVA: I cannot explain, I cannot describe this sensation.

VIPPER: Was this sensation something frightful...?

DIAKONOVA: Yes, yes.

VIPPER: What did you feel, an arm, a leg, a human body? What frightened you? What is frightening about touching something hard? Perhaps you had heard about the murder?

DIAKONOVA: No, I hadn't heard about it.

VIPPER: So you had the sensation that your leg hit against a body? And this set off such panic in you?

DIAKONOVA: I got frightened and woke up.

1. Cherniakova was a mutual acquaintance of Cheberiak and Diakonova.

2. THE CASE AGAINST BEILIS

Document 22: An Eminent Psychiatrist Supports the Ritual Murder Accusation

Ivan Sikorskii was a well-known psychiatrist who served as an expert witness for the prosecution. During the initial investigation of Andrei's murder in May 1911, Sikorskii offered the following assessment of the crime, asserting that it had all the hallmarks of a ritual murder and intimating that Jews had committed the crime.

Source: Ludwig Rosenberger Collection 450 D/5. Special Collections Research Center of the Regenstein Library at the University of Chicago. Spelling has been changed for consistency.

As in the case direct facts pointing to the nationality of the murderers are wanting, one has to confine himself to considerations of an historical and anthropological character, and before everything else, to answer the questions to whether a crime like the assassination of Iushchinskii ought to be regarded as a mere accident, or, on the contrary, as a criminal anthropological type, manifesting itself in different degrees in particular cases. It is imperative to recognize the latter alternative as true, i.e., it must be assumed that murders committed in the same way as that of Iushchinskii recur from time to time in Russia, as well as in other countries that rank high in civilization. The assassination of Iushchinskii appears as a most typical and absolutely complete case, in which three main features, viz., the slow bleeding, the torturing and the subsequent killing of the victim, are distinctly stamped in this case in their full scope and in regular order. In this typical crime the last act, i.e., the killing, only takes place after the victim has been made use of for the two previous acts. . . . There is no room for doubts either in the Velizh case, or in that of Kiev as to the peculiar kind and the characteristics of the dastardly deed. This criminal anthropological phenomenon must be recognized as an undisputed fact that occurs from time to time in one country or another. One must admit, with the anthropological criminologists, that the psychological basis of crimes of that type is sought in racial revenge or—to use the expression of the well-known opponent of antisemitism, Leroy Beaulieu—in the "Vendetta of the Sons of Jacob." The typical similarity of this vendetta, and of its manifestations in all countries, may be accounted for by the fact that the nationality that produces this crime is interspersed among other nationalities, where it carries with it the traits of racial psychology. It must be admitted in addition to the above that the killing of Iushchinskii as well as the similar murders cannot be explained entirely from the point of view of racial vindictiveness, which only accounts to some extent for the torturing and killing of members of a different race, while it fails to explain the reason why the attempts are directed against infants and juveniles, as well as the evacuating of the blood of the doomed victim. This peculiarity, no doubt, requires other explanations and a special expert investigation, all the more so, as the dastardly murders of children bear the character of a malignant tradition that evidently does not show any tendency to disappear.

Document 23: Aron Beilis Appeals on Behalf of His Brother

Mendel Beilis was not permitted to see anyone or consult with legal counsel after his arrest. It was only after his indictment in January 1912 that Beilis met for the first time with lawyers who had agreed to serve as his defense team. In a letter written in December 1911, Aron Beilis asked the authorities to investigate whether or not his brother Mendel had received two letters sent the previous month.

Source: *Derzhavnyi arkiv Kyïvs'koi oblasti* (State Archive of Kiev Region, hereafter DAKO), *fond* (record group) 183, *opis'* (archival invenstory) 5, *delo* (file) 4, *listy* (pages) 121–121 *oborot* (verso). Excerpted from the microfilm collection "Beilis Case Papers," copyright East View Information Services.

To the Procurator of the Circuit Court

It is already the fifth month that my brother Mendel Beilis has been in prison. Cut off from the entire world, from kin and close ones, he does not know . . . all the rights given to prisoners by the law. It is possible that he fails to realize the exact charge against him.

My brother has not been permitted to meet with me or any other relative as well as those close to him. Prompted by the natural desire to inform my unfortunate brother that he has the right to file a complaint for the actions of the investigating magistrate and can also request to summon witnesses and experts to refute the accusation, I set forth in my two letters addressed to him at the prison in Kiev, according to the advice of those well versed in such matters, what he needs to do. In the letter from November 11th I advised my brother to address a complaint to the Circuit Court regarding the investigation and his arrest, and to request the dismissal of charges because of his innocence.

In the letter from November 17th I informed my brother to submit an application to interrogate . . . Professor of Oriental Studies Kokovtsev about the problem of so-called ritual murders. I also suggested to my brother to petition the investigating magistrate to inquire about the findings of the Medical Council in Petersburg—the highest medical institution in the country—about the nature of the wounds found on the body of Andrei Iushchinskii.

As far as I know, no complaint or petition has been filed by my brother with the Circuit Court. I have also not received any kind of answer to my letters from my brother.

This leaves me to suppose one of two things: Either my brother did not understand what I wrote him or, more likely, my letters are being held back somewhere and have not reached the person for whom they are intended. . . .

I am requesting that Your Excellency, in the name of the law and pity for my powerless brother, take . . . measures to clarify whether my letters reached my brother. I am also petitioning for permission to meet with my brother in the presence of officials who would guarantee that my conversation with my brother would be limited to information permitted by the law regarding his defense against the accusation.

Document 24: Beilis Describes His Life in Prison

In 1926 Beilis published the English version of his memoirs in which he discusses the physical discomfort and mental anguish he endured in prison.

Source: Mendel Beilis, *The Story of My Sufferings*. New York: Mendel Beilis Publishing Company, 1926. Pp. 62–64 and 79. Spelling has been changed for consistency.

On a day in January 1912, I was summoned to the district court to get my indictment. My joy was boundless. Come what might, I was glad to know where I stood, to know for certain that I was condemned.

I was escorted to the district court. I was dressed in a Russian red-brown sheepskin and had shoes without soles. In the court I found my wife and brother whom I had not seen for a long time. We could not talk to each other, however. In the morning before going to court I received a letter from my wife and brother telling me that I should announce in court that I had retained as my lawyers Messrs. Gruzenberg, Grigor'evich-Barskii and Margolin.

I was handed the indictment. When I realized its contents I was stunned. I was not charged overtly with "ritual murder." I was nevertheless accused of having murdered Iushchinskii or having been accomplice to his murder with others. I was charged in accordance with the statute dealing with premeditated murder, the death of the victim having been caused by bodily tortures inflicted upon it, or the victim having been subjected before murder to cruel torment. The statute called in case of conviction for 15–20 years imprisonment with hard labor (*katorga*).

Of course, had the investigation been carried on along the lines of an ordinary criminal case, the indictment would have been only a sort of a personal "frame-up," a libel. Since, however, the investigation and the whole case in general had been undertaken with the intention of turning it into a "ritual" murder case—the whole case became a "frame-up" on the Jewish people. I was amazed at Fenenko.[1] He told me that he was not indicting me, and yet he composed the indictment. As I was later informed he had intended at first to quash it, since there was no proof whatever against me. That is what he himself said—but the Prosecuting Attorney of the Kiev district court, together with the notorious Zamyslovskii and the whole band of Black Hundreds compelled Fenenko to formulate the indictment. It should be borne in mind that Fenenko did not even intend to arrest me. All that was done by the procurator Chaplinskii. Nevertheless, the "higher powers" were far from being satisfied with the indictment. Its premises were weak at their foundation....

Heart-broken, I was led back to my dark and dingy prison. About that time I began to feel my feet swelling—they were covered with sores. Since my shoes had no soles, the walking on the snow and ice caused me intense suffering. Hence the swelling and sores. The pain was almost unbearable. The skin burst and blood was oozing through. I did not find much sympathy for my sufferings on the part of those around me.

One morning I asked the doctor to be brought in to examine me. I was in agony. The officials were merciful enough and sent me a "feldscher" (surgeon's aide). The feldscher looked at the sores and said that I was to be transferred to the hospital. Later a guard came in and shouted—"hurry up, let us go." I could not move, however; my feet were so swollen that I could not stand up. He did not want to listen to any reason and kept shouting, "Move on."

One of the prisoners who happened to be in the hall brought some rags and wrapped them around my knees. And in this manner, crawling on my knees over the snow and ice, I dragged myself to the hospital. In the hospital I encountered another feldscher, who had lived . . . not far from our factory. When he recognized me, he became pale and trembled from pity and amazement. He ordered at once that I be undressed and given a warm bath. I was afterwards given clean linen and put into a warm, clean bed. This produced such a beneficial effect that I slept on uninterruptedly for thirty-six hours. . . .

After the good rest I had, an operation was performed upon me. My friend the feldscher was not present—I was operated on by the physician. When he commenced to open the sores, the pain made me wince and scream. The doctor smiled and observed, "Well, Beilis, now you know for yourself how it feels to be cut up. You can imagine now how Andriusha had felt when you were stabbing him and drawing his blood—all for the sake of your religion." You can imagine how cheerful I felt at this raillery of the doctor. He kept on cutting leisurely and I had to bite my lips not to let myself scream. . . .

The first year of my imprisonment had drawn to its close. My prison cell was far from being comfortable—the walls were plastered with cement, and during the winter frost they always had an icy coating. The heating was insufficient. During the warmer days the lime on the walls would thaw and the walls would be dripping with moisture. The dripping from the ceiling made it impossible for me to sleep. I was dressed in the usual prison garb, i.e. a shirt of sack linen and a long coat of raggy cloth. I had to wear my shirts for stretches of two and three months. There was no lack of the usual cooties. In the prison itself the mortality from typhoid fever was about six or seven men per day. This was in no way surprising in view of the extraordinary filth, the disgusting food, the unheated rooms (not infrequently during the frosts I used to find my hand frozen to the ice on the wall). All these things made a perfect breeding ground for various epidemics.

1. Fenenko was investigating magistrate.

Document 25: Police Official Points to Vera
Cheberiak as the Guilty Party

*In February 1912 Aleksandr F. Shredel, head of the gendarmes[1] in Kiev
Province, submitted a report indicating that Vera Cheberiak and her
gang were the likely murderers of Andrei.*

Source: "Tsarskoe pravitel'stvo i protsess Beilisa," *Krasnyi arkhiv,* vol. 45
(1932): 166–168.

Chief of the Kiev Provincial Gendarmes A. Shredel to Vice-Director of
Department of Police, N. P. Kharlamov, February 14, 1912.

Top secret

In response to your letter of February 9th, I have the honor to report to
Your Excellency that the preliminary investigation regarding the murder
of Andrei Iushchinskii in Kiev is fully complete, and that after confirma-
tion of the act of indictment by the Kiev Palace of Justice the case was
transmitted to the 12th Branch of the Kiev Circuit Court. Twenty-four witnesses have been summoned by the prosecution and 150 by the defense. In
addition, both parties have summoned a considerable number of experts.

The case will probably come to trial in April or May of this year, and
the trial will last about ten days.

At the present time, further inquiries into the murder of Andrei
Iushchinskii are being conducted exclusively by my assistant, Lieutenant-Colonel Pavel Ivanov with the participation of Kirichenko, a police
inspector. These inquiries are mainly concentrated on the wife of a postal
clerk, Vera Vladimirovna Cheberiak, known to Your Excellency, and on
professional criminals closely associated with her, the majority of whom
have been deprived of rights or condemned to hard labor. They are: Ivan
Latyshev, Nikolai Mandzelevskii, Petr Singaevskii, Porfiry Lisunov,
Pavel Mosiak, Vekenty Mikhalkevich, and Boris Rudzinskii.

An entire series of burglaries that took place in Kiev by members
of this band has recently been discovered; they also robbed two stores
selling firearms.

It is interesting to observe that, since the murder of the boy Iushchinskii, the burglaries have completely stopped as well as the visits of

the above-named burglars to Cheberiak's home, probably the result of inquiries into the Iushchinskii case and some preliminary arrests.

It is likely that the boy Iushchinskii was an involuntary witness to one of the criminal acts of this gang, and that "it was necessary to do away with him out of fear."

Now each burglary committed by the members of the gang is being investigated in detail and, as the facts of the case are clarified, the investigations of . . . Kirichenko are sent to the court authorities.

Considering the insufficiency of the evidence against Mendel Beilis and the general interest in the case, which is well known in Europe, the accusation of Mendel Beilis in the murder of Andrei Iushchinskii may cause a great deal of unpleasantness to judicial officials and may lead to a justified rebuke for the hastiness of their conclusions, even the one-sidedness exhibited during the investigation.

1. The gendarmes were a special branch of the police responsible for state security and other law enforcement duties.

Document 26: Police Official Stresses the Lack of Credible Evidence against Beilis

One month after reporting his suspicions of Vera Cheberiak and her gang, Aleksandr Shredel submitted another report that reiterated his earlier observation that the evidence against Beilis was flimsy. He predicted that the case against Beilis would collapse due to the overwhelming weakness of the state's case.

Source: "Tsarskoe pravitel'stvo i protsess Beilisa," *Krasnyi arkhiv,* vol. 45 (1932): 168–170.

Chief of the Kiev Provincial Gendarmes A. Shredl to Vice-Director of Department of Police, N. P. Kharlamov, March 14, 1912.

Top secret

In response to your letter of March 5th, No. 62, I have the honor to report to Your Excellency that the correspondence from Kiev published on February 25th in the newspaper *Rech'* (Speech) regarding the Beilis case is seemingly based on the fact that during the middle of February of this year the procurator of the Kiev Superior Court received from the ministry of justice an order to remit on February 21st copies of all records of the investigation concerning Beilis. This order created a series of rumors and opinions that the ministry of justice had received information about the complete absence of evidence against Beilis. But such rumors are apparently without basis, and the copies of all records of the investigation regarding Beilis are necessary for Assistant Procurator Vipper of the St. Petersburg Palace of Justice, who . . . will appear at the Beilis case as the chief prosecutor.

I want to add that it is now clear that the circumstantial evidence gathered against Beilis will completely fall apart at the trial. As Your Excellency himself has found in the preliminary investigation, the main witnesses against Beilis are the lamplighter Shakhovskii and his wife. . . . Shakhovskii now declares that he will testify at the trial that on March 12, 1911, at 8 o'clock in the morning, he saw Andrei Iushchinskii on the Lukianovka, near Cheberiak's apartment; and that Evgenii Cheberiak, now deceased, told him that he had seen some man resembling Beilis, on March 12th, seize Iushchinskii and drag him toward the property of Zaitsev. He does not know anything more about the case. The wife of Shakhovskii categorically declares that she does not know anything about the case, and that she gave information regarding Beilis after Detective Vygranov got her drunk. . . .

A secret investigation has recently been conducted into the connections of the wife of the postal clerk Cheberiak and members of the criminal world. During this investigation an entire series of burglaries, which occurred in the city of Kiev between the end of February to the middle of March of the past year, came to light. The participants in these thefts were discovered at the same time, and an entire series of such cases was transmitted to the judicial authorities. The discovery of these thefts must undoubtedly be ascribed to the skillful and energetic activities of the Kiev Police Captain Evtikhii Kirichenko. This is why I considered it my duty to bring to the attention of the Kiev Governor the useful activity of Kirichenko, so as to encourage his service and zeal.

By excluding all those criminals who, on March 12, 1911, could not have taken part in the murder of Iushchinskii because they were at that time either in prison or not in Kiev, we must concentrate the investigation on the activities of the professional criminals Ivan Latyshev, Boris Rudzinskii, sentenced to hard labor, and also Petr Singaevskii, who is at liberty.

.... Their testimony is so contradictory that it is necessary to subject it to the most careful analysis. The investigation has quite definitely disclosed that on March 13th of the past year, i.e., on the day after the murder of Iushchinskii, the above-named persons boarded an express train for Moscow, where they were all arrested on March 16th in a beer hall because their appearance and behavior aroused the suspicion of local detectives.

Document 27: Psychiatrist
Rebuts Sikorskii's Claim

Sikorskii's claims did not go unchallenged. Vladimir P. Serbskii, the preeminent forensic psychiatrist in the Russian Empire, criticized Sikorskii for violating norms of scientific inquiry.

Source: Alexander Tager, *The Decay of Czarism: The Beilis Trial.*
Philadelphia: The Jewish Publication Society of America, 1935. P. 50.

Jewish ritual accusations never appear in places where the Christians do not believe beforehand in the existence of ritual murders among Jews. The same is true here as in stories of ghosts or phantoms: they appear only where they are believed in.... Sikorskii undoubtedly transgressed the limits of objective judgment and was directed by thoughts that sprang from his unbridled imagination and not from a cold and critically thoughtful intellect.... Sikorskii's narration can be utilized perhaps for a work of fiction, but beyond this, it has no significance....

It is not a psychiatric conclusion and does not, therefore, contain material for criticism from the psychiatric point of view. After reading this expert conclusion, we even began to doubt that its author was a psychiatrist.... The same person who has earned scientific merit by his study of religious deliriums and trances of numerous individuals and masses appears to have himself succumbed to the influence of such a benighted prejudice. To use the verbiage of Sikorskii himself, his expert conclusion is not an incidental or simple mistake, but a "complicated and deliberate misdeed, thoroughly thought out and executed in accordance with a prepared plan."

Document 28: International Uproar against the
Blood Libel and Prosecution of Beilis

Prominent gentile academics, politicians, clerics, and theologians in Germany and England protested the prosecution of Beilis for ritual murder, which they insisted had no place in civilized society.

Source: *Kieff Ritual Murder Accusation: Protests from Leading Christians in Europe.* London: Jewish Chronicle and Jewish Tribune, 1913. Pp. 12–16; and *London Times* (May 6, 1912): 7. Spelling has been changed for consistency.

German Protest: On March 12, 1911, the boy Andrew Iushchinskii was murdered at Kiev. In spite of every effort, no convincing evidence of the authorship of the crime has yet been discovered. A Jew has, however, been arrested and charged, and the inquiry against him is now in progress.

Whether this Jew is the murderer we cannot judge. It would not be proper to anticipate a judicial decision in a case that is still pending, especially when it is being tried in another country.

But there is one aspect of the case that compels us in accordance with our consciences to adopt a certain attitude.

Mob agitators have eagerly seized on the crime, and have boldly asserted that the boy Iushchinskii was slaughtered by Jews in order to drain his blood and use it for ritual purposes, in obedience to an alleged Jewish religious law. This unscrupulous fiction, spread among the people, has from the Middle Ages until recent times led to terrible consequences. It has incited the ignorant masses to outrage and massacre, and has driven misguided crowds to pollute themselves with the innocent blood of their Jewish fellow men. And yet not a shadow of proof has ever been adduced to justify this crazy belief. The most esteemed Christian authorities on Jewish literature have proved incontrovertibly that the Jews have never been exhorted by their religion to murder their fellow men.

We deem it is the duty of everyone to whose heart the moral progress of mankind is dear to raise his voice against such deplorable absurdities. We thus join in the protest of the most esteemed Russian scholars, authors, and artists, believing that such a protest should not be limited by frontiers, but should concern the heart of the whole civilized world.

English Protest: We want to associate ourselves with the protests signed in Russia, France and Germany by leading Christian Theologians, Men of Letters, Scientists, Politicians and others against the attempt made in the City of Kiev to revive the hideous charge of Ritual Murder—known as the "Blood Accusation"—against Judaism and the Jewish people.

Animated by the sincerest friendship for Russia, we can have no idea of meddling with the domestic concerns of that country. Much less do we wish to prejudice in the slightest degree the course of the criminal trial with which this accusation has become identified. In the terms of the published protest of our Russian colleagues and friends and in their intimation that they welcome support from other countries, we have the best assurances that our motives will not be misinterpreted.

The question is one of humanity, civilization and truth. The "Blood Accusation" is a relic of the days of Witchcraft and Black Magic, a cruel and utterly baseless libel on Judaism, an insult to Western culture and a dishonor to the Churches in whose name it has been falsely formulated by ignorant fanatics. Religious minorities other than the Jews, such as the Early Christians, the Quakers, and Christian Missionaries in China, have been victimized by it. It has been denounced by the best men of all ages and creeds. The Popes, the Founders of the Reformation, the Caliph of Islam, Statesmen of every country, together with all the great seats of learning in Europe, have publicly repudiated it.

It is the more necessary that these testimonies should be renewed because, among the ignorant and inflammable populace of Eastern Europe, the "Blood Accusation" has often given rise to terrible outbreaks of mob violence against the Jews, and there is grave reason to fear that its present resuscitation may endanger many innocent lives in the crowded Jewries of the Russian Empire.

Document 29: Public Protest against the Prosecution of Beilis

The indictment and prosecution of Beilis for ritual murder prompted an outcry of protest by prominent intellectuals throughout the Russian Empire. Vladimir Korolenko, a well-known writer, journalist, and political activist, wrote the following appeal.

Source: *Kieff Ritual Murder Accusation: Protests from Leading Christians in Europe.* London: Jewish Chronicle and Jewish Tribune, 1913. Pp. 18–20. Spelling has been changed for consistency.

To the Russian Public

In the name of justice, reason and humanity we raise our voices against this new outbreak of fanaticism and black mendacity.

The eternal struggle of humanity on behalf of liberty, legal equality, and fraternity, and against slavery, hate, and social discord, has been with us from ancient times. And in our time, as always, the same persons who uphold the outlawed condition of their own people are the most persistent to excite among them the spirit of religious and racial enmity. While they have no consideration for popular opinion, or popular rights, which they are ready to suppress by the severest measures, they flatter popular prejudices, fan the flames of superstition, and incite to deeds of violence against their country men of other races.

In connection with the still uninvestigated murder of the boy Iushchinskii at Kiev, the false story of the use of Christian blood by Jews has been sown and broadcast once more among the people. This is a familiar device of ancient fanaticism. In the early ages AD the pagan priests used to accuse the Christians of partaking of the Communion with the blood and flesh of a pagan infant killed for the purpose, and in that dark way explained the mystery of the Eucharist. Thus it was that this dark and malicious legend arose. The first blood shed on its account by the prejudiced sentences of Roman judges and amid the shouts of the ignorant pagan crowd, was the blood of Christians. And the first to disprove it were the Fathers and the teachers of the Christian Church. "Be ashamed"—wrote St. Justin the Martyr, in his address to the Roman Senate—"be ashamed to attribute such crimes to men who are not concerned in them. Stay! Come to your senses!." . . .

By this time the falsity of the legend that accused the early Christians is as clear as noonday. But, invented by hate, adopted by blind ignorance, the absurd invention did not die out. It has become an instrument of enmity and dissension even among Christians themselves. It has gone so far that in some places a Roman Catholic majority will cast the accusation upon the Lutherans, while a majority of the latter will brand with it the Roman Catholics.

But the greatest sufferers from this fiction are the Jews who are scattered among other nations. The *pogroms* caused by it have drawn a trail of blood through the dark history of the Middle Ages. At all time murders happen, the motives and authorship of which are a source of perplexity. Where there is a Jewish population it is a simple matter to explain such crimes by the alleged ritual use of blood. Such a thing excites ignorant superstition, and thus influences the evidence of witnesses, deprives the judges of calmness and impartiality, and leads to judicial errors and *pogroms*.

Frequently the truth has eventually come to light, though too late. Sensible and just men would then be seized by shame and indignation. Many Popes and spiritual and secular rulers have branded the malicious superstition and forbidden the authorities to lend to its investigation a religious meaning. Among us such a ukase was issued on March 18, 1817, by the Emperor Alexander I, and was confirmed on January 30, 1835, in the reign of the Emperor Nicholas I. In 1870 the Greek Patriarch Gregory also condemned the blood legend applied to the Jews, and declared it to be a "disgusting prejudice of men infirm in their faith."

But ukases are moldering in State archives, while superstitions skulk abroad, and now the old lie, fraught with violence and *pogroms*, is being circulated again, even from the tribune of the State Duma. In this lie there is the ring of the same malice that once incited the blind pagan crowd against the early followers of the Christian doctrine. Not long ago in China, where Chinese priests circulated the same fable about the use of infant by the missionaries, it cost the lives of hundreds of Christians and Europeans. Dark and criminal passions always follow in its train, while it always tends to blind the populace and pervert justice.

But the sentiments of love and truth must always combat it. The words of St. Justin the Martyr do not apply to the Roman Senate alone.

"Be ashamed; be ashamed to ascribe such a crime to men who are not concerned in it. Stay! Come to your senses!"

We join our voices to this holy Christian voice, whose appeal to love and reason rings through the depth of ages.

Fear those who sow falsely. Believe not the black lie that has so often made itself red with blood, killing some, and covering others with sin and shame.

Document 30: Chaplinskii Defends Decision
to Pursue the Case against Beilis

Georgii G. Chaplinskii deflected accusations that he was ignoring the evidence against Vera Cheberiak and her gang. In May 1912 he explained to his superior at the ministry of justice that he would not submit to pressure to cease his investigation of Beilis.

Source: "Tsarskoe pravitel'stvo i protsess Beilisa," *Krasnyi arkhiv*, vol. 45 (1932): 172–173.

I am submitting to the Minister a report on the case of Iushchinskii in which I give my reasons for ignoring the declarations of Brazul'-Brushkovskii. The information given by him is confused, patently absurd, and is calculated to obscure the facts of the case. My view is that the judiciary cannot be a toy in the hands of all kinds of swindlers and must not return cases for additional investigation on patently absurd grounds. However, since many court officials . . . have a different opinion, and maintain that any new information, no matter how absurd, must receive attention according to article 549 of the criminal code statutes, I considered it my duty to report to the Minister about my order on this subject in detail, so that if His High Excellency should not share my view, he may order me to transmit the information given by Brazul'-Brushkovskii to the consideration of the courts.

This is a very unfortunate matter, and great pressure is being brought to bear on all sides. Many reputable persons are trying to persuade me that the Beilis case should be discontinued. . . .

Naturally, I am not taking this bait and am driving away my well-wishers. . . .

Do not fail to communicate my report in detail to the Minister. This report will have enormous significance for him because my refusal to return the case for further inquiry will elicit an uproar in the kike press.

Document 31: Antisemites in Kiev Commemorate the Death of Iushchinskii

The Dvuglavyi orel (The Double-Headed Eagle) marked the anniversary of Andrei's death with articles about his "martyrdom" and ritual murder. The following poem appeared on the second anniversary of his death.

Source: "Poem to Andriusha Iushchinskii," *Dvuglavyi orel*
(*The Double-Headed Eagle*), no. 8 (March 13, 1913): 1.

Two years have passed since the Jews,
Having gathered as a *kahal*[1] family,
Decided to commit an act of fanaticism
And become rich with the blood of a youth.
How Ianenka[2] grabbed you
And lured you to the cave
And performed terrible torments
And pricked you with an awl
Your blood spilled over,
Blood oozed from your head,
The kike *kahal* was enraptured
And sang hymns to Jehovah.
They collected your blood
Into bottles they poured it
And celebrated Passover with blood,
With Russian blood, the blood of Andriusha.
There are many such monsters,
And many vampires among the kike,
As examples for their offspring/descendants
They pour Christian blood into matzo.

1. The *kahal* was the communal organization that governed the internal affairs of a Jewish community and represented its interests to the secular authorities. In the eyes of the *Dvuglavyi orel* (The Double-Headed Eagle) the kahal was the nerve center of the purported Jewish conspiracy to subvert Russian society.

2. Ianenka is the diminutive of Jan. However, nobody with that name was involved in the Beilis case.

3. THE TRIAL

Document 32: The Indictment

The government charged Beilis with the murder of Andrei and claimed that he worked with unknown accomplices who planned the murder for religious reasons. The indictment stated that "religious fanaticism" prompted the killing.

Source: *Delo Beilisa: Stenograficheskii otchet.* Volume 1. Kiev, 1913. P. 37.

On the basis of the aforementioned information, Menachem-Mendel Tevye Beilis, age 39 and resident of the town of Vasil'kov in the Province of Kiev, is accused of agreeing with unknown persons to willfully deprive the twelve-year-old boy Andrei Iushchinskii of his life because of religious fanaticism. The murder took place on March 12, 1911 on the premises of the Zaitsev brick factory, located on Upper Iurovskii Street in the city of Kiev. Beilis seized Iushchinskii, who was playing there with other children, and led him to the factory, where Beilis's accomplices, with his knowledge and consent, bound Iushchinksii's arms, gagged him, and then killed him by stabbing him with a sharp implement . . . on his head, neck, and torso, causing wounds to the cerebral vein, jugular veins and arteries on the left temple as well as wounds to the cranium, liver, right kidney, lungs, and heart. The wounds were accompanied by painful and prolonged suffering and the body's nearly full loss of blood. . . .

Document 33: Revolutionaries Call for a Day of Protest

Parties across the political spectrum turned their attention to the Beilis trial and used the event to galvanize either support of or opposition to the autocracy. The major Marxist organization in Kiev tried to organize a one-day strike in support of Beilis.

Source: DAKO, *fond* 2, *opis'* 228, *delo* 264, *list* 85. Excerpted from the microfilm collection "Beilis Case Papers," copyright East View Information Services.

Russian Social-Democratic Workers Party!

Workers of all countries, unite!

Comrades! The Beilis affair has riveted the attention of the entire world. The entire world is protesting against the accusation of ritual murder, against the accusation of Jewish cannibalism, against lawyers invoking crude superstitions.

Our voice, the voice of the working class of Russia needs to be especially strong and ring out in a common voice of protest. Together with the working class of the whole world we long ago announced a struggle with exploitation and any kind of oppression, particularly national oppression. Together with Russian democracy we understand well that tsarism's bloody policy wants to split us into enemy camps. Workers of many cities—Riga, Warsaw, Petersburg, Vilna and others—have answered in fitting manner the foul and false accusation with strikes and other forms of protest. It is your turn, workers of Kiev, to reveal the savage violence of the tsarist regime and its servants, the Black Hundreds.

Comrades! Let Friday, October 4th be our day of united protest, when we do not go to work and loudly announce:

Long Live the One-Day Strike of Protest!

Long Live the Unity of Workers of the Whole World!

Down with Tsarism and Its Bloody Policies!

Long Live the Russian Revolution!

Long Live the R.S.D.W.P.

Document 34: Government Efforts to Maintain Calm in Kiev

Officials in Kiev were concerned that political parties would try to stir up trouble between Jews and non-Jews through leaflets and newspaper articles. In certain cases officials threatened newspaper editors with arrest for publishing articles that sought to disturb law and order.

Source: DAKO *fond* 2, *opis* 229, *delo* 264, *listy* 123–124. Excerpted from the microfilm collection "Beilis Case Papers," copyright East View Information Services.

October 12, 1913

In today's issue of the newspaper the *Double-Headed Eagle* (no. 31) published in Kiev, there is an article "Listen, Russian Land" about ritual murders among Jews that is written in an extremely tendentious tone and stirs up the Russian populace against Jews.

In light of this article and its tendentious tone and arousing character that threatens the preservation of order, especially at the present time during the hearing of the Beilis case, I have taken measures not to permit the printing of similar articles and, having refrained for tactical considerations from inflicting upon the editor of the *Double-Headed Eagle,* a penalty required by decree. . . . I have limited myself to inviting the editor to meet with me and warned him that he will be subject to the extreme penalty of arrest for three months . . . if a similar article appears in the newspaper. The editor of the *Double-Headed Eagle* declared that the article was reprinted from Issue no. 6115 of the *Kazanskii Telegraf* (The Kazan Telegraph) from October 6. . . .

Document 35: "The Eternal Fairy Tale"

Even newspapers that were not affiliated with any political party had an interest in the trial. In this editorial a middle-of-the-road paper worried that the ritual murder accusation could disrupt social calm throughout the country.

Source: *Narodnaia kopeika* (The People's Kopek), no. 124 (October 17, 1913).

The eternal fairy tale—this is the libel against the Jews, the vile libel that is known as ritual murder. The libel, which is appreciated only by the ears of those for whom it is important—sows darkness and ignorance. The newspapers have brought to us a new fact asserting the old truth about the libel against the Jews.

The other day in the city of Orel there was unsettling news about the apparent murder by Jews of Anatoly Rostovtsev, the twelve-year-old son of . . . the owner of a wine shop. After a long search, the boy was found and it turned out that the entire story was made up. The boy's coat was ripped up, but it turned out that his classmates had ripped the coat.

True, the lie surfaced and was exposed. But the Jewish population of Orel experienced a tense moment.... And they should be glad that the truth came to light so quickly....

Can we guarantee that tomorrow such a vile libel will not flare up in another place?

No, there are no guarantees.

Up to now, while there is still darkness and ignorance among us, we cannot offer any guarantees.

And the eternal fairy tale will ... remain in the mean time an eternal fairy tale.

A stupid, eternal fairy tale.

Document 36: Conservative Newspaper Appeals for Restraint

Even though most conservative newspapers believed that Beilis was guilty, some acted responsibly by appealing to its readers to behave in a lawful manner and not engage in anti-Jewish violence.

Source: *Russkoe znamia* (The Russian Banner), no. 239 (October 24, 1913): 1.

Jewdom knows very well that our victory will bring about incalculable damages and losses for the Jewish community in Russia and abroad. ... It would be very strange if the community did not take all measures and possibilities to disrupt this victory. We already remarked on and clarified such attempts in Kiev that ended in failure thanks to the restraint and composure of the very patient Russian people.... It is a foreboding of the moral victory of Orthodoxy over Satanism, Christianity over the Talmud, and the Russian people over the so-called "oppressed people." ...

The pogrom, as we have already warned our readers and like-minded people many times, presents the greatest evil for Russia and the Russian people, and we, standing firmly on the ground of the strictest law and order and carrying out the word of the adored Autocracy, ... caution the Russian people to avoid even the smallest illegal action or display of illegitimate actions.

The duty of every honest Black Hundred, patriot, loyal Russian person ... is to bear firmly in mind that any illegal action against the kikes in connection with the Iushchinskii affair will undermine patriotic Russian politics and betray the Motherland. This serious, historical moment calls for calm, restraint, and self-possession from the population.

Document 37: Letter Describes the Killing of Andrei

The public displayed a keen interest in Andrei's death as evidenced by the dozens of letters sent to government officials involved in the prosecution of Beilis. The letters indicated the deep roots that the blood libel had in late Imperial Russian society.

Source: DAKO *fond* 183, *opis'* 5, *delo* 4, *listy* 178–181. Excerpted from the microfilm collection "Beilis Case Papers," copyright East View Information Services.

Conversations with people who saw Iushchinskii's corpse, information from the press, and photographs of the deceased have led me to think that Iushchinskii died without suffering. The opinion that he did suffer is not only mistaken but is a reason why investigators have been forced to rummage through a muddle of facts, the majority of which have almost no significance, to waste energy on revealing the links and causal relationships among the facts, and to spend time on purely technical work that is not connected to the essence of the matter.

The death of Iushchinskii was not agonizing; . . . and blood did not flow from the body but was sucked out by a special instrument or instruments. I am certain of this because of the following: 1) there were no signs of force on Iushchinskii's body while he was alive; 2) there was no coagulation of blood on the body, head and wounds; and 3) Iuschinskii's cap was pierced with some kind of awl with the obvious aim of putting the police on a false track. . . . The doctors who performed the autopsy were surprised by the artistry with which the piercings were made. There were stabs to the arteries, but not one of the arteries was punctured, that is, no hemorrhaging was found in the muscle tissue.

A fatal blow to the heart was the cause of death, . . . The body was thrown somewhere soft, and so there were abrasions and bruising on the body. Consequently, Iushchinskii was killed in a place that was prepared for the murder. The embroidered rag found in Iushchinskii's pocket was

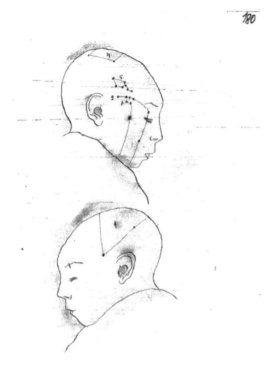

Drawing of Andrei's corpse
with stab wounds. "Beilis
Case Papers," copyright
East View Information
Services, 2005.

placed there with the aim . . . of leading the investigation on the wrong
track.

Exsanguination of the body was caused by forty-seven wounds,
which supports the opinion that the wounds . . . were the result of torture.
The wounded artery was the source of the blood splatter; it is also known
that wounds to the artery do not hurt while blood is flowing from it. It
is clear that the murderers or murderer of Iushchinskii did not intend to
make him suffer. . . .

As a result of tedious, painstaking work, which I carried out only on
the basis of photographs and a list of all the wounds and where they were
inflicted. . . . I have created the following drawing of Iushchinskii's body.

On the right temple . . . is *Ursa Major* (David's Chariot or the Seven
Bulls of the Heavenly Pasture, which was the ancient name of this constel-
lation). Eleven wounds on the right temple, right side of the head, right
cheek and right side of the neck . . . faithfully depict *Draco*; four piercings
on the right lung, right cheek, and right side of the neck form *Aries* (the

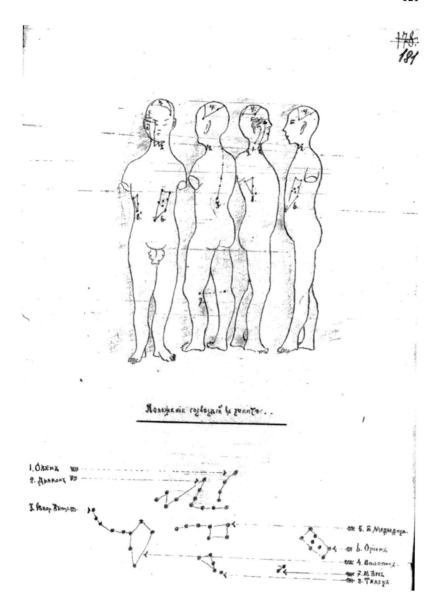

Pattern of wounds in the shape of constellations. "Beilis Case Papers,"
copyright East View Information Services, 2005.

sign of the month of March). One piercing on the left lung and four on the head form the *Ploughman*. One wound on the neck . . . and four along the spine depict the *Northern Corona*, and five wounds on the right side of the body is *Taurus* (the sign of the month of April). Seven wounds in the area of the heart and one wound below the navel form *Orion* and two wounds beneath the kneecaps depict *Canis Minor*. There are forty-seven stars in the constellations. I am firm in my conviction that my general conclusion is correct. But I wanted a thorough verification. When Detective Polishchuk approached me and asked me to prepare a summary of the material on the Iushchinskii case collected by him for Lieutenant-Colonel Ivanov, I agreed to do so on the condition that he acquire for me a copy of the autopsy report.

In Polishchuk's report . . . there was one piece of information that corroborated my conclusions, namely that the deceased Iushchinskii on the eve of his death was . . . rushing about with the thought of seeing his father.

He did not believe that his father had been killed in the war and was convinced that he would soon see him. . . . A certain Bunimov[1] . . . lived with Beilis. He was the son of a butcher and he assured the boy that he served in the war with Iushchinskii's father. He also assured the boy that his father was still alive and that he—Bunimov—would help him see his father. In light of this and being sure that without me the case would not take the correct track, I decided to wait before I announced my findings so as not to hurt the pride of all the professionals who labored diligently and complicate what was already a complicated case. Lieutenant Colonel Ivanov paid attention to only part of the information reported by Polishchuk, . . . Then Polishchuk was fired and Inspector Kirichenko began to conduct the investigation and wander completely from the correct track. . . .

In light of this I find it immoral to be silent about what I know and think about the Iushchinskii case and have decided to present to Your Excellency an account of the case for your consideration.

1. No one by that name appears in any of the trial documents.

Document 38: Hypnosis Will Reveal the Murderer

Letter writers drew upon their experience with mysticism, the occult, and spiritualism to help the prosecution determine whether or not Beilis was guilty. The author of this letter claimed that hypnosis would ascertain whether Beilis or Vera Cheberiak was responsible for Andrei's death.

Source: DAKO, *fond* 864, *opis'* 10, *delo* 33, *listy* 1–1 *ob*. Excerpted from the microfilm collection "Beilis Case Papers," copyright East View Information Services.

It is with great sorrow that I am convinced that the Beilis affair will remain unsolved and the unfortunate boy will not be avenged. It seems to me that in these situations, when people . . . find it difficult to get to the truth, the science of Hypnosis is called for. Would it really be illegal if some doctor or professor would publicly place Cheberiak and Beilis under hypnosis . . . ? Certainly it is not necessary to tell anyone about this since the kikes would be able to concoct something and suggest to the defendant to say something that was not true. If Beilis is not guilty, then this is his good fortune. They will acquit him. But if he is guilty and judged as such what an insult to God if he were to be free. And Cheberiak—she will again continue with her tricks and will also be free. It is a terrible pity! Good gracious! I wish you all the success in punishing the villains.

Document 39: Séances Confirm Beilis's Guilt

Many letter writers turned to fortunetellers, clairvoyants, and other spiritual advisors in order to learn the name of Iushchinskii's murderer. Some even claimed that they spoke with the spirit of Iushchinskii in their efforts to find out what happened.

Source: DAKO, *fond* 864, *opis'* 10, *delo* 39, *listy* 10–10 *ob*. Excerpted from the microfilm collection "Beilis Case Papers," copyright East View Information Services.

If you are interested in the murder of Iushchinskii, we learned its details from answers to our questions that we asked through the means of spiritualism.

OCTOBER 17, SÉANCE 1: We asked "Who killed you?" by using the medium of a saucer.[1] Answer: Beilis and Zhokman killed me, they grabbed me, stabbed me with a lance, and made matzo with the blood. Beilis then threw me into the cave. . . .

OCTOBER 18, SÉANCE 2: Tell us all the details.

ANSWER: Beilis and Zhokman captured me, Beilis killed me, and they stabbed me with a lance, the blood was scarlet red, they ate matzo. Beilis and Zhokman threw me into the cave, I lay there for a month and a half, they hid my shoes in the barn, my pants and cap are at Beilis's, . . . please be so kind as to write my relatives, for which I'll be grateful. . . .

After this we asked where we could find Zhokman. Zhokman is at the Black Sea. . . .

OCTOBER 19, SÉANCE 3: Questions on where he was killed, which of your things are stored and where they are hidden, where is Zhokman.

QUESTION: We asked for the second time where his things were.

ANSWER: They are in the basement on shelves filled with clay and a lot of blood and please write to mommy . . . that they killed me at Beilis's (illegible).

We are not signing our names because you can verify for yourself everything that is described above regarding those involved in ritual murder and where his things are stored or were stored. You can do so with the means we used or you can go to any society of Spiritualists.

1. The saucer is presumably an early version of a Ouija board.

Document 40: *New York Times* Condemns Tsarist Regime

The press in Europe and the United States followed the trial closely and reported on developments in the Kiev courtroom. This New York Times' *editorial criticized the Russian government for countenancing antisemitism.*

Source: *New York Times* (October 9, 1913), 12.

The Czar on Trial

In Kiev, Russia, yesterday, there was placed on trial, behind closed doors, one MENDEL, charged with the murder of a Russian lad, IUSH-CHINSKY, in 1911. BEILIS is a Jew, and is accused of "ritual murder," that is to say of having killed a boy to get his blood for alleged use in the rites of the Jewish religion. There are two elements in this case that make it of great importance and interest to right-thinking persons in all parts of the world.

One is the clear presumption, on all available official Russian testimony, of the entire innocence of the accused. Immediately after the murder of the boy, M. MINSCHUK,[1] Chief of the Detective Service in Kiev, with several assistants, investigated the case and reported, first, that there was no evidence against BEILIS, the accused, and, second, that the boy was murdered by a gang of criminals whom he was suspected of betraying. For this report M. MINSCHUK was accused of manufacturing evidence to hinder the prosecution and to protect Jews, and though acquitted in one trial, was retried and condemned to prison for a year, with his assistants. The fact clearly discredits the whole case of the prosecution.

The second significant fact in the case is the nature of the accusation, the allegation of murder for Jewish ritual purposes. The crime does not and cannot exist. It has been shown over and again, and long ago, that there is nothing in the religious belief or practice of the Jews that remotely requires or sanctions or suggests the thing charged. Strict and searching inquiry by eminent men of science, theologians, historians, physicians, not Jews, in Great Britain, in Germany, in France, has resulted in the distinct and unqualified verdict that the belief in this crime has not the slightest foundation in fact, and that it is a foolish, blind superstition, bred of prejudice upon ignorance.

It has so been held and denounced by the Pope, by the head of the Orthodox Church, by living Bishops of that Church, and by a Czar of Russia, Alexander I, in 1817, confirmed by Nicholas I in 1835. What renders this base and baseless accusation more revolting at this late day, and by the officials of a Government professedly Christian, is the fact that it is in the twentieth century the revival of a device used by pagans in the first century to justify the oppression and slaughter of Christians. The Government of Russia, and especially the Czar of Russia, the authoritative head of a great branch of the Christian Church . . . is 2,000 years behind the times.

For the Russian peasants who are the helpless victims of this superstition, and who accept it like a superstition was accepted by the half savage crowds of the Roman Arena, we can have pity, and even with the brutal action inspired by it we can have patience. But for educated men, particularly for Russian officials who deliberately appeal to the superstitious and incite to brutal action, we can have only indignant detestation. And that feeling is nowise affected by the fact that this outrage is directed to those of one or another race, one or another religion. The outrage is upon humanity.

Every humane, every decently human instinct condemns it. It is true that the offense is one that cannot be dealt with in the ordinary ways of international communication, though it is by no means wholly beyond them, as was very properly shown in the case of Rumania as conducted by the late Secretary HAY.[2] But in the court of public opinion such an offense can and must be dealt with. Fortunately there is a large number of educated and fair-minded Russians who not only will recognize the jurisdiction of that court and respect its verdict, but will contribute to it. And this element in Russia is bound to gain in strength and influence.... If the ... trial at Kiev results in the conviction of the hapless BEILIS, and that is followed by the disorders it is calculated to produce, this element will be not weakened, but reinforced. In view of this fact and of the general protest that has been aroused it may be said that the Czar and autocracy are now on trial.

1. Mishchuk.

2. As Secretary of State (1898–1905), John Hay defended Jews in Romania, which was obliged by international treaty to respect the rights of Jews as citizens.

Document 41: Kazimir Shakhovskii Reveals that the Police Scripted His Testimony

Kazimir Shakhovskii was a drunkard whose ever-changing testimony was the result of the police badgering and instructing him what to say.

Source: *Delo Beilisa: Stenograficheskii otchet.* Volume 1. Kiev, 1913. Pp. 173–175.

VIPPER: Did you go to the cave to take a look after Andriusha's body was found?

SHAKHOVSKII: No.

VIPPER: Why?

SHAKHOVSKII: I didn't have time.

VIPPER: But everybody went to take a look.

SHAKHOVSKII: There were a lot of people and then they took the body away.

VIPPER: You knew that they had found the body of Andriusha, but you were not curious to find out whether or not it was really Andriusha?

SHAKHOVSKII: No.

VIPPER: When the body of Andriusha was found, did you say anything to a detective or someone else?

SHAKHOVSKII: No.

VIPPER: You didn't say to one of the detectives . . . that you had seen Andriusha on March 12th?

SHAKHOVSKII: Exactly so, I told Detective Krasovskii.

VIPPER: Did you tell him right after Andriusha was found or was it in May or June that you first mentioned it?

SHAKHOVSKII is silent.

VIPPER: You don't remember?

SHAKHOVSKII: I don't remember. . . .

VIPPER: Did you see Zhenia after the body was found?

SHAKHOVSKII: Yes, I saw him.

VIPPER: In all likelihood you asked what Andriusha had been doing or where he was headed?

SHAKHOVSKII: About three or four days later.

VIPPER: Did he tell you something about where they had been?

SHAKHOVSKII: He said that they had walked around the Zaitsev grounds.

VIPPER: What else did he say?

SHAKHOVSKII: That they had been chased away from there.

VIPPER: Who chased them away?

SHAKHOVSKII: An unknown man.

VIPPER: Did he describe to you the appearance of this unknown man? Did he say that the man had a beard?

SHAKHOVSKII: Not at all. He simply said that an unknown man had chased them away.

VIPPER: Did you not tell the investigator about this because they could pin it on you?

SHAKHOVSKII is silent.

VIPPER: Were you afraid?

SHAKHOVSKII: Of course. They could have smacked me around.

SHAKHOVSKII: He (Zhenia, ed.) said that some man had chased them.

SHMAKOV: Did he not say that this man was Beilis?

SHAKHOVSKII: He didn't say so.

SHMAKOV: He didn't say that this man had a black beard?

SHAKHOVSKII: He didn't say so.

SHMAKOV: But you yourself told the investigator that Mendel was the only person with a black beard living there at the time. Did you testify to this?

SHAKHOVSKII: Yes, I did. . . . I can't say.

SHMAKOV: Are you denying this?

SHAKHOVSKII: No. Perhaps I said this.

SHMAKOV: You alluded to the fact that they beat you. Who beat you? What was the reason for beating you?

SHAKHOVSKII: I don't know. They called me a "blight."

SHMAKOV: And what does this mean?

SHAKHOVSKII is silent.

SHMAKOV: Did they accuse you of talking too much and warned you to hold your tongue?

SHAKHOVSKII is silent.

SHMAKOV: What was the reason for beating you?

SHAKHOVSKII: It concerned what I said.

SHMAKOV: Concerned what, Beilis?

SHAKHOVSKII: I can't say.

SHMAKOV: Are you saying that they beat you and explained to you why?

SHAKHOVSKII: They didn't explain anything. They only gave me a good thrashing.

SHMAKOV: Are you saying that eight men struck you?

SHAKHOVSKII: Yes, . . .

SHMAKOV: This means that you do not know who beat you?

SHAKHOVSKII: I don't know. One was tall and dark.

SHMAKOV: Why are you afraid to testify if you do not know why they beat you? . . . Why did you conclude that they beat you on account of the Beilis matter? You are under oath and must tell the truth. Why did they call you a "blight?"

SHAKHOVSKII: Yes, I swore an oath.

SHMAKOV: Did you not tell your wife at that time that Zhenia and An-driusha rode on the clay grinder?

SHAKHOVSKII is silent.

SHMAKOV: You didn't tell her about Beilis?

SHAKHOVSKII is silent. . . .

NIKOLAI B. KARABCHEVSKII (defense attorney): Did you first say that on March 12th you saw the deceased Iushchinskii with Zhenia Cheberiak? Then you said that people began to frighten you and someone struck you. Were these people Jews or Russians?

SHAKHOVSKII: Russians.

KARABCHEVSKII: Were they from Cheberiak's circle?

SHAKHOVSKII: Perhaps they were, but I don't know.

KARABCHEVSKII: In any event, they were not Jews?

SHAKHOVSKII: Not Jews.

Document 42: Iuliana Shakhovskaia is Unable to Offer a Consistent Account

Like her husband, Iuliana Shakhovskaia was unable to provide a consistent account of what she knew about the murder. Her testimony revealed the underlying weakness of the government's case against Beilis.

Source: *Delo Beilisa: Stenograficheskii otchet.* Volume 1. Kiev, 1913. Pp. 190–191 and 193–196.

VIPPER: Did you meet an old woman who goes by the name Wolf-Woman?

SHAKHOVSKAIA: I was lighting the lamps and she was walking by. . . . She said something to me while she was walking by, but I cannot remember what she said. . . .

VIPPER: You are not able to remember anything of the conversation?

SHAKHOVSKAIA: She was drunk. She said something to me, but I was in a rush and lit the lamp quickly because I was running late.

VIPPER: Did you tell this to anyone or did Polishchuk make inquiries?

SHAKHOVSKAIA: Polishchuk questioned me.

VIPPER: When he was asking the questions, did he give you something to drink?

SHAKHOVSKAIA: Vodka. . . .

VIPPER: When did Wolf-Woman tell you that she saw Beilis drag Andriusha? Where did she see this?

SHAKHOVSKAIA: I don't remember too well what she told me. . . .

VIPPER: Where did she see Beilis drag Andriusha?

SHAKHOVSKAIA: Yes.

VIPPPER: Or can't you remember?

SHAKHOVSKAIA is silent.

VIPPER: Tell me, did your husband tell you anything?

SHAKHOVSKAIA: Nothing.

VIPPER: Excuse me, he didn't tell you anything about seeing Andriusha on Saturday, the last time with Zhenia? He didn't speak to you about this?

SHAKHOVSKAIA: He didn't.

VIPPER: But didn't he at least say something about this?

SHAKHOVSKAIA: No. . . .

VIPPER: In general, are you afraid to say that you saw Andriusha with Zhenia on Saturday?

SHAKHOVSKAIA: Yes, I saw him.

VIPPER: Did you tell everyone?

SHAKHOVSKAIA: I didn't tell anyone.

VIPPER: And when was the first time you told someone that you saw Andriusha with Zhenia on Saturday?

SHAKHOVSKAIA: I didn't tell anyone.

VIPPER: So how did the detective find out?

SHAKHOVSKAIA: I told Vygranov, and he told the detective.

VIPPER: And how did it come about that Vygranov found out from you?

SHAKHOVSKAIA: Because they approached us, gave us vodka, but we didn't know anything. They all gave us vodka.

VIPPER: And before Vygranov you didn't tell anyone?

SHAKHOVSKAIA: No.

VIPPER: But you nevertheless testified, I must remind you that you are under oath, that you saw all of this.

SHAKHOVSKAIA: Yes. . . .

SHMAKOV: Did you see these two boys Andriusha and Zhenia?

SHAKHOVSKAIA: I saw them.

SHMAKOV: But you didn't see them when you walked away?

SHAKHOVSKAIA: I didn't see them when I walked away.

SHMAKOV: Yet you told the detective that you also saw them when you were walking away. . . .

SHMAKOV: Didn't you say that Wolf-Woman had told you that she had met a man carrying Andriusha? Didn't Wolf-Woman describe a man with a black beard?

SHAKHOVSKAIA: Yes, a man with a black beard.

SHMAKOV: Did she not say that this was Mendel Beilis, the clerk at the Zaitsev factory?

SHAKOVSKAIA is silent.

SHMAKOV: Did she not say that he took Andriusha . . . and carried him somewhere?

SHAKHOVSKAIA: No.

SHMAKOV: And you do not remember if she told you that a man with a black beard carried him off? What are you playing at here? Didn't Wolf-Woman convey this to you?

SHAKHOVSKAIA: No. . . .

GRUZENBERG: Previously you told the investigator that Mendel was the person who dragged the boy. This is not true? Wolf-Woman didn't tell you this?

SHAKHOVSKAIA: Yes, she didn't tell me.

KARABCHEVSKII: . . . Polishchuk said that you and your husband saw how Mendel Beilis and his son dragged the boy to the oven. Did Polishchuk say this?

SHAKHOVSKAIA: Yes, he did.

KARABCHEVSKII: But you didn't tell him this?

SHAKHOVSKAIA: No, I didn't tell him.

ZARUDNYI: You were so interested in the murder of Iushchinksii that when you met Wolf-Woman the first word from you was about the incident. But when Wolf-Woman told you that she saw how they dragged the deceased Iushchinskii, you were not interested. Why didn't you announce this important circumstance to anyone? Did you ask her about it?

SHAKHOVSKAIA: No.

ZARUDNYI: And why didn't you inform someone about this before the detective had come to see you?

SHAKHOVSKAIA is silent.

BOLDYREV: Why didn't you provide information about this? You told about it only when the police inquired? Why didn't you make a declaration right away?

SHAKHOVSKAIA: I did.

BOLDYREV: You told about it, but not on that day?

SHAKHOVSKAIA: I told everyone on that day, I told various people. . . .

VIPPER: At first you testified as if Wolf-Woman herself saw how Beilis dragged Andriusha, but the second time you testified that she herself didn't see him do so, but only knew about it. When you testified the first time as if she herself saw him, you had already had a conversation with the detective?

SHAKHOVSKAIA: Yes.

VIPPER: Did they get you drunk and promise you some kind of reward?

SHAKHOVSKAIA: Certainly they promised me something. . . . Certainly they said that there will be a reward. . . . Both times they promised a reward. . . .

BOLDYREV: You are saying that before you met the investigator the first time, the detectives persuaded you to testify as to the truth and promised you something?

SHAKHOVSKAIA: Yes.

BOLDYREV: Did they tell you what to testify to or did they say, testify about what you know?

SHAKHOVSKAIA: Yes, they said, testify about what you know.

BOLDYREV: Did they tell you what to say?

SHAKHOVSKAIA: Yes.

BOLDYREV: When you went to the inspector the second time, did the detectives talk with you again?

SHAKHOVSKAIA: Yes.

BOLDYREV: What did they say?

SHAKHOVSKAIA: They told me what I say in my testimony.

BOLDYREV: And they said that it was necessary to testify against Mendel?

SHAKHOVSKAIA: They said so, everyone said so.

BOLDYREV: What did they say?

SHAKHOVSKAIA: They told me what Mendel did....

BOLDYREV: Witness, clarify the following: did the detectives tell you what to say or did you tell the detectives that Wolf-Woman told you that she saw Mendel dragging the boy to the cave? When you informed the detectives about this, did they tell you to inform the investigator about all this? Or did you say nothing to the detectives and the detectives themselves told you to testify against Mendel, even though Wolf-Woman said nothing to you.

SHAKHOVSKAIA: Yes, yes, they said that.

BOLDYREV: Did you or did you not tell the detectives about Mendel?

SHAKHOVSKAIA: No, I did not.

BOLDYREV: And so the detectives told you?

SHAKHOVSKAIA: They told me.

BOLDYREV: And what did you tell the detectives?

SHAKHOVSKAIA: I didn't tell them anything....

VIPPER: Aren't you afraid to testify and help convict someone based on the word of someone else, on the basis of Wolf-Woman's word? Indeed, you testified against Beilis! Do you understand what kind of responsibility you are assuming by doing this?

SHAKHOVSKAIA: I didn't say anything about Mendel.

VIPPER: Well then, does this mean that you didn't tell the truth when you talked about him?

SHAKHOVSKAIA: No, I didn't say anything about this!

VIPPER: Does this mean that you made up what you said about Mendel to the detectives...?

SHAKHOVSKAIA: Whatever, I'll testify against this person....

Document 43: Wolf-Woman Contradicts the Testimony of Iuliana Shakhovskaia

Anna Zakharova, also known as Wolf-Woman, offered testimony that contradicted the statements given by Iuliana Shakhovskaia and served only to weaken the state's case.

Source: *Delo Beililsa: Stenograficheskii otchet.* Volume 1. Kiev, 1913.
P. 222.

BOLDYREV: Remember that you are under oath and have to tell the
truth. Tell us what you know about this case.

ZAKHAROVA is silent.

VIPPER: You have mentioned Iuliana Shakhovskaia. Do you know
Iuliana?

ZAKHAROVA: I know her.

VIPPER: Have you ever spoken with Iuliana?

ZAKHAROVA: I spoke with her when we ran into each other. . . .

VIPPER: Do you remember when the boy Andriusha was killed, when
they found his body?

ZAKHAROVA: I heard about it, but I don't know who killed him. . . .

VIPPER: So what did you talk about with Iuliana? Were you drunk?

ZAKHAROVA is silent.

VIPPER: Do you drink?

ZAKHAROVA: I drink a little bit.

VIPPER: Were you drunk when you talked with Iuliana? Perhaps you
were running at the mouth?

ZAKHAROVA: Yes, perhaps.

VIPPER: What did you discuss with her? Idle chatter?

ZAKHAROVA: We just began to talk. . . .

VIPPER: Did the detectives question you?

ZAKHAROVA: Yes, they asked if I had spoken with Iuliana. I said that I
didn't say anything, that I didn't know anything.

VIPPER: And so Iuliana made up the conversation?

ZAKHAROVA: Yes, she made it up.

VIPPER: And you aren't making up anything?

ZAKHAROVA: No.

VIPPER: Do you like to jabber when you drink?

ZAKHAROVA: No, I don't like to.

VIPPER: Do you like to talk or to be silent?

ZAKHAROVA: I like being silent more than talking.

Document 44: Iuliana Shakhovskaia Tells
that the Police Coached Her

In additional testimony Iuliana Shakhovskaia reiterated that the police had told her what to say in order to incriminate Beilis. In the following selection Shakhovskaia admitted that a detective fabricated for her the details of what Wolf-Woman supposedly told her.

Source: *Delo Beilisa: Stenograficheskii otchet.* Volume 1. Kiev, 1913. Pp. 96 and 222.

SHMAKOV: I want to ask a question of the witness. Did Wolf-Woman tell you about the man with the beard in the presence of the boy Nikolai Kaliuzhnyi?[1]

SHAKHOVSKAIA: Yes.

SHMAKOV: ... Did the detective tell you what to say as testimony or did you decide for yourself?

SHAKHOVSKAIA: By myself.

SHMAKOV: You consequently stated that Wolf-Woman told this and that to you and in the presence of the boy Nikolai Kaliuzhnyi. I am asking you whether the detectives coached you to refer to Nikolai Kaliuzhnyi?

SHAKOVSKAIA: Yes, the detectives coached me.

SHMAKOV: And they also coached Nikolai Kaliuzhnyi?

SHAKHOVSKAIA: Yes....

1. See Document 45.

Document 45: A Young Boy Denies the Testimony
of Iuliana Shakhovskaia and Wolf-Woman

Shakhovskaia and Wolf-Woman claimed that a boy by the name of Nikolai Kaliuzhnyi witnessed their conversation about a man with a black beard who dragged Andrei across the yard at the brick works. While Kaliuzhnyi did not deny meeting both women, he testified that he did not hear what they said to each other.

Source: *Delo Beililsa: Stenograficheskii otchet.* Volume 1. Kiev, 1913. P. 222.

BOLDYREV: Look at this woman and say if you know her.

KALIUZHNYI: I know her.

BOLDYREV: Where did you see her?

KALIUZHNYI: On Polianka St.

BOLDYREV: Who else was there?

KALIUZHNYI: Iuliana Shakhovskaia....

BOLDYREV (To Shakhovskaia): She is Zakharova, the same woman about which you were speaking and who told you about the man with the black beard who dragged the boy?

SHAKHOVSKAIA: Yes, she's the one.

KALIUZHNYI: Zakharova and Shakhovskaia spoke between themselves. I couldn't hear what they were saying. They were laughing.

VIPPER: I would like to know what the witness Zakharova wants to say now....

ZAKHAROVA: That I don't know why she is saying this about me.

BOLDYREV: Witness Shakhovskaia, do you affirm that she told you that she saw a man with a black beard drag the boy?

SHAKHOVSKAIA: Yes.

BOLDYREV: And you, Wolf-Woman, you say that you didn't tell her this?

ZAKHAROVA: Yes.

BOLDYREV: And you, Shakhovskaia, do you affirm that she was drunk?

SHAKHOVSKAIA: Yes.

Document 46: Criminal States that One Member of Troika Confessed to the Murder

In July 1912 Amzor E. Karaev told Nikolai Krasovskii that Petr Singaevskii, a member of the troika, admitted his involvement in the murder of Andrei. His statement was entered in the trial record.

Source: *Delo Beilisa: Stenograficheskii otchet.* Volume 2. Kiev, 1913. Pp. 4–6.

KARAEV: Plis[1] told me that he had heard a lot of good things about me. I told him that I had a serious matter to discuss with him.... He asked what kind of money I was talking about, and I said forty thousand rubles. Then he asked whether the matter would be "dry" or "wet," which in criminal jargon means "without murder" or "with murder." I told him that it might be necessary to kill about ten people, and that we would need men who did not waver. He said with regret that it was a pity that Bor'ka and Latyshev were not here. When I asked who is Bor'ka, Plis answered, "Rudzinskii." When I asked where they were, Plis answered that they had already been sentenced to hard labor[2].... He announced that Andrei Iushchinskii had been killed in Vera Cheberiak's apartment. I then said that in all likelihood somebody had ratted on them. To this Plis answered that two sisters, whose name he did not know, had apparently testified that they were at Vera's place and saw how Latyshev, Bor'ka Rudzinskii and he, Plis, ran from one room to another and how Latyshev covered something with a raincoat in the corner. In response to the sisters' question, Vera said that the raincoat was covering ... stolen goods.... I then expressed the thought that the sisters could pose a threat, and he told me that Vera had gone to see them for this reason and warned them not to say anything, threatening ... to prove that one of the sisters had buried her child in a ... garden. I told Plis that Makhalin was my comrade whom he could trust as he trusts me. Then I asked Plis if he had made up his mind and if I could tell everything to Makhalin. Plis answered in the affirmative. Then I addressed Makhalin while pointing to Plis, "Here is the real murderer of Iushchinskii, together with Vera Cheberiak, Rudzinskii, and Latyshev." I then turned to Plis and asked if that was so, and he answered, "Yes, it was our doing."

1. Plis was the code name of Singaevskii used by Krasovskii and Karaev.

2. Rudzinskii had been sentenced to three years in prison for his role in the March 12th robbery. Latyshev committed suicide by jumping out a window in police headquarters after he was brought back to Kiev from Moscow for questioning in the March 12th robbery.

Document 47: Vera Cheberiak's
Testimony Is Challenged

*Georgii Chaplinskii worked with Vera Cheberiak after the withdrawal
of the first indictment in May 1912 to assemble new testimony that
would strengthen the government's case. One critical piece of additional evidence was Cheberiak's assertion in mid-1912 that her son
Zhenia had told her one year earlier that Beilis had chased and seized
Zhenia. During questioning it became clear that her testimony was
inconsistent, indicating that she had made up the details of the conversation between herself and Zhenia.*[1]

Source: *Delo Beilisa: Stenograficheskii otchet.* Volume 1. Kiev, 1913. Pp.
304–305, 308–309, and 315–316.

VERA CHEBERIAK: Krasovskii and Vygranov came by and said, "Your
boy must be shown the cave." I asked Zhenia, "Can you recall if
someone chased Andrei?" He thought a bit and remembered. "Yes,"
he said, "there was such an incident!" I said, "Tell us about it," and
he said, "It was in the morning. Mama went to the market, Papa was
at work, and we were alone. Andrei came and we went for a walk."
They were joined by the two Nakonechnyi girls and another girl,
and they all went to the revolving clay grinder within the factory
grounds. Zhenia said that when they sat down—he on one side,
Andrei on the other . . . the two Beilis boys were also there along
with two other boys. They started chasing each other, and the boys
started throwing stones. . . . At some point Beilis grabbed Zhenia by
one hand and Andrei with the other. Zhenia was slim and dexter-
ous and managed to wiggle out and run away, but Andrei couldn't
manage to. . . . I don't remember what happened to Andrei. . . .

BOLDYREV: Zhenia told you all this?

CHEBERIAK: Yes, to me and my husband.

BOLDYREV: Did the investigators ask you why you didn't say anything
about this incident?

CHEBERIAK: Because the children had been chased repeatedly but
there never was an incident when they were dragged. When they
started questioning Zhenia, he recalled the incident. . . .

VIPPER: When your children started telling you about the incident at the Zaitsev factory, did you tell them, "You better keep quiet and not blab?"

CHEBERIAK: No, I didn't. . . .

VIPPER: Andrei was found dead in March, but Zhenia told you about Beilis only in June?

CHEBERIAK: Yes. . . .

VIPPER: That is, before your first arrest?

CHEBERIAK: Yes.

VIPPER: So Zhenia told you about the last minutes of Andriusha's life. Why didn't you feel it was necessary . . . to announce that you knew all this?

CHEBERIAK: Zhenia didn't tell me about the incident before my arrest, but after my release.

VIPPER: When were you first arrested?

CHEBERIAK: In July.

VIPPER: Zhenia told you about the incident after you were released the first time?

CHEBERIAK: Yes.

VIPPER: You remember this well? . . . Do you affirm that the children said nothing to you before the arrest?

CHEBERIAK: They said nothing. . . .

KARABCHEVSKII: The witness has forgotten a great deal, and there are contradictions with previous testimony. I therefore request that the previous testimony be made public. . . .

BOLDYREV: Witness, we will read part of your previous testimony, and you will explain the contradictions: The witness was interrogated on June 24, 1911, and testified, "When Iushchinskii's body was found, Zhenia told me the same day, 'You see, Mama, I told you what Fyodor said to me about the kikes slaughtering Andrei'." I then questioned Zhenia about the last time he was with Andriusha Iushchinskii, and Zhenia replied that Andriusha Iushchinskii came to see him about three weeks before his body was discovered. . . . They met on the street around 3:00 PM. Andrei asked Zhenia to go for a walk with him but Zhenia declined. That's all Zhenia told me.

BOLDYREV: This is what you testified to on June 24, 1911. Why did you change your testimony? You said Zhenia met Andrei on the street and that it was 2:00 PM.

CHEBERIAK: That's what Zhenia told me.

BOLDYREV: The witness was also questioned on April 22, 1911, and testified, "I haven't seen Andriusha since he moved to Slobodka. If he moved in May of last year, that would mean that I haven't seen him for almost a year. But my son Zhenia told me that about four weeks, maybe a little less, before his body was discovered Andrei came over and . . . suggested that they go for a walk to the place where he was subsequently found dead. I wasn't home at the time, and Zhenia didn't want to leave the apartment unlocked and therefore he didn't go with him. . . . According to Zhenia, it was approximately 2:00 PM. However, Zhenia didn't tell me about Andriusha dropping by at the time and revealed this incident after Andrei's body was discovered. I recall asking Zhenia if Andrei had come around to Lukianovka at any time since his parents moved to Slobodka, and Zhenia said that shortly after they moved, Andrei came over several times and they took walks in the fall of last year."

GRUZENBERG: When you were interrogated the first time, you testified that Zhenia told you, "I haven't seen Andriusha since he moved to Slobodka."

BOLDYREV: This was your first testimony. Please clarify for us why you testified as you did. . . . In your . . . interrogation in April, you testified differently.

CHEBERIAK: Because this is what Zhenia told me.

BOLDYREV: You better tell the truth. . . .

CHEBERIAK: No, this is what Zhenia told me.

BOLDYREV: Remember that you are under oath.

CHEBERIAK: I remember, but that's what Zhenia told me.

1. Vera also rehearsed her youngest child Liudmila to back up the testimony regarding Beilis seizing Andrei. Liudmila claimed that two Jews were with Beilis on the morning of March 12, 1911, but she broke down in tears when her friend Dunya confronted her and denied her account.

Document 48: Vasilii Cheberiak Is Caught in a Lie

At the trial it was revealed that Vasilii Cheberiak was at work on March 12, 1911, when his son Zhenia purportedly told him about Beilis seizing Andrei earlier that morning. He also could not explain his failure to inform the police at the time of the murder about the two men who supposedly helped Beilis. Cheberiak's testimony lent credence to defense assertions that he had made up the story (probably at the behest of his wife) about Zhenia claiming that he had seen Beilis seize Andrei.

Source: *Delo Beilisa: Stenograficheskii otchet.* Volume 1. Kiev, 1913. Pp. 318, 320, and 328–329.

VASILII CHEBERIAK: I was home. Suddenly my son Zhenia appeared at the door, all pale. I asked, "What's wrong?" He said they were all playing on the factory grounds when the kike Mendel and two others started chasing them and grabbed Zhenia and Andriusha Iushchinskii. My son managed to tear himself away and escape. I don't know what happened to Andriusha Iushchinskii.

BOLDYREV: This is what your son told you? When did you speak with him?

CHEBERIAK: On that very day. All my children were playing on the factory grounds, along with two other girls. The smallest one . . . who was also weaker than the others, was left behind and saw how Mendel dragged Andriusha toward the kiln.

BOLDYREV: Who saw this?

CHEBERIAK: My younger daughter and son.

BOLDYREV: And your son told you about this?

CHEBERIAK: Yes. . . .

BOLDYREV: So he came running and told you about riding on the clay grinder and Beilis grabbing Andriusha?

CHEBERIAK: Beilis and two other kikes who by his description seemed to be rabbis or *tsaddiks*.[1] He said they didn't look like the ones he usually saw on the street; they were new faces.

BOLDYREV: Did he say if the Beilis boy was there?

CHEBERIAK: The Beilis family was also there.

BOLDYREV: Did you attach importance to this incident?

CHEBERIAK: Yes, I did, because there were previous instances when Jews grabbed Christian children.

BOLDYREV: You took particular notice of this right away when Zhenia told you, or when it all came to light?

CHEBERIAK: I warned him not to go to the Zaitsev grounds. I ordered him not to. . . .

BOLDYREV: Why didn't you report this to the authorities when the body was discovered?

CHEBERIAK: At that time it had not been announced that the body had been discovered.

BOLDYREV: But afterwards, once the body was found and it became public, why didn't you tell the authorities what Zhenia had told you?

CHEBERIAK: For some time I didn't know about the murder. . . . I told Krasovskii, Mishchuk and others when they came by to ask me questions. . . .

GRUZENBERG: I am asking if you remember how long you were at work on March 12?

CHEBERIAK: No, I don't remember.

GRUZENBERG: Do you know that your supervisor told the investigator the precise hours you were on duty on that date?

CHEBERIAK: No.

GRUZENBERG: Perhaps you remember that on the twelfth you were on duty from 9:00 AM to 3:00 PM?

CHEBERIAK: I don't remember.

GRUZENBERG: You don't remember? Tell me this, then, how long does it take you to walk from your apartment to work?

CHEBERIAK: About twenty-five minutes. . . .

GRUZENBERG: Let me repeat my question. . . . You testified on December 20, 1911. Until then detectives constantly bothered your wife—she was interrogated six times, was called six times for hearings before the examiner. Did you tell her, "Tell the authorities what happened, that two Jews grabbed and dragged the boy." Did you or did you not say this in the course of eleven months?

CHEBERIAK is silent.

BOLDYREV: Why didn't you say anything?

CHEBERIAK: I didn't say anything because she herself knew about it.

GRUZENBERG: Really, a Jew and two rabbis grab a Christian boy who perishes. Why didn't you report such Jewish fanaticism?

CHEBERIAK: I didn't pay attention. . . .

GRUZENBERG: Yesterday you said that Zhenia calmly told you that when they were riding on the clay grinder Mendel Beilis and two rabbis rushed up and dragged Andriusha off. But in your testimony from December 20, 1911, there was not a word about any rabbis. You also didn't say anything about someone grabbing and dragging Andriusha, only that Mendel Beilis chased after him and Beilis's children laughed. You didn't know where Andriusha went. How do you explain that you said this to the investigator?

CHEBERIAK: I told the investigator that Zhenia and Andriusha Iushchinskii rode on the clay grinder. But my Zhenia stated that he broke loose, and the Jews dragged Andriusha in the direction of the kiln.

GRUZENBERG: . . . Yesterday you said that the Jews seized Andriusha and . . . you didn't say a word where Andriusha went. You said you didn't know where Andriusha ran.

CHEBERIAK: I remember it now.

GRUZENBERG: Was Zhenia already dead when you spoke with the investigator? Didn't he die on August 8th?

CHEBERIAK: Yes.

GRUZENBERG: And you talked with the investigator in December. . . . On December 20th you gave testimony . . . without speaking one word about rabbis. You have testified that Zhenia died on August 8. This means that you testified several months after his death. From where did you receive new information if Zhenia had already died? You alluded to Zhenia as the source.

CHEBERIAK is silent. . . .

BOLDYREV: They interrogated you on December 20th and you didn't say anything about rabbis. Now you are saying that Zhenia let you know that Beilis grabbed Andriusha by the arm and that two other Jewish rabbis were also there. . . . It is of interest to the court and defense to explain why there are such contradictions in your testimony. Why do you now testify differently from what you testified at the preliminary investigation on December 20th?

1. *Tsaddiks* (plural) were spiritual leaders of Hasidic sects.

Document 49: Vera Cheberiak Tries to Solicit False Testimony

*Realizing that she needed to bolster her testimony about Zhenia tell-
ing her that he and the other children had seen Beilis seize Andrei on
March 12, 1911, Vera Cheberiak took the bold and desperate action to
solicit perjured testimony from a young boy by the name of Zarutskii
who was waiting to testify about what he witnessed that day.*

Source: *Delo Beilisa: Stenograficheskii otchet.* Volume 1. Kiev, 1913. P. 368.

BOLDYREV: Witness Vera Cheberiak, . . . the boy says that you put him
up to testify that he was at the clay grinder at that time.

CHEBERIAK: Liuda, Zhenia, and Valia told me that he was at the clay
grinder. Liuda asked that he not forget that he rode on the clay
grinder at that time. Liuda talked with him, but I never instructed
him. Let the boy look me in the eye and say that I instructed him
to say this.

BOLDYREV: Tell us, boy, what happened.

ZARUTSKII: She was sitting on the bench and called over to me.

CHEBERIAK interrupts: A lot of people were sitting there.

BOLDYREV: Please, do not prompt him.

ZARUTSKII: She called to me and said, "Don't you remember how you
were playing with Zhenia, Liuda, Valia, and Andrei and how Beilis
grabbed them? Zhenia and Valia broke free and ran away, but Andriusha was unable to do so and Beilis dragged him off."

CHEBERIAK: Liuda said that, not I. You are lying? This is unseemly.

BOLDYREV: Please, do not steamroll over him. Didn't you ask the
boy, "Don't you remember how you rode on the clay grinder with
Andrisha and Zhenia and how Beilis rushed out and grabbed them"?

CHEBERIAK: It was Liuda who said this, not me.

Document 50: Vera Cheberiak Accuses the
Jewish Community of Attempted Bribery

*Vera Cheberiak hoped to use the journalist Stepan Brazul'-Brush-
kovskii to divert attention away from her involvement in the murder.
She used their trip to Kharkov as part of a ploy to accuse the Jewish
community of plotting to win the acquittal of Beilis.*

Source: *Delo Beilisa: Stenograficheskii otchet.* Volume 1. Kiev, 1913. Pp. 306–307.

CHEBERIAK: Krasovskii showed up and said, "Vera Vladimirovna, you must help us. You were illegally arrested, your children were poisoned, and you, as a mother, should receive exacting vengeance for your children." I said, "How can I help you?" He answered, "Only if you want to, but if you don't help us then your husband will lose his job and things will be bad for you." . . . A little bit after this he told me, "I am taking you to see an acquaintance who is an influential gentleman who will reveal to you everything about the matter—why your children were poisoned and why you were arrested." He came again on December 6th and invited me to go with him. . . . I asked, "Where to?" He said, "To Kharkov." I agreed and he took me to Kharkov, and we stayed in an expensive hotel room. I don't remember how much it cost. . . . Once we arrived in Kharkov, he told me that this gentleman will ask you questions, . . . Brazul' said that the gentleman was a member of the State Duma in St. Petersburg. The gentleman asked me to tell him about my arrest. I started telling him about the arrest . . . and he interrupted me, saying "Everything you are telling me I already know. Tell me how Zhenia died." I started to tell him about Zhenia's death and then about Beilis. The gentleman said to me, "Don't talk about Beilis. Stop talking about him. You will say what I am telling you, namely that criminal elements may have killed Zhenia. Nothing about Beilis." . . . I said, "What do you want from me?" "We will do for you whatever you desire if you take responsibility for the matter."

BOLDYREV: What matter?

CHEBERIAK: To take responsibility for the matter. I said, "I don't understand what I should take upon myself," and he told me, "The murder." "How can I," I said, "take responsibility for the murder if I did not do it?" He said, "This is not our concern. Just take responsibility for it." "How can I do so? How can a woman commit murder?" . . . He said, "We will take care of everything only if you agree. . . . You only have to sign a piece of paper and then you will receive documents so you can go." I said, "Why me?" He said,

"You're appropriate since Zhenia was Andrei's friend. No one else
is more appropriate than you."... I said, "If I take the blame, what
happens next?" He said that if I am arrested the very best lawyers
will defend me and I will have nothing to worry about.... Then two
other gentlemen entered the room.... One of them said, "We will
give you 40,000 rubles and travel documents. You will go abroad
and everything will be okay. If you delay in taking responsibility, it
will be too late. Now is the most appropriate time to help us."... I
said, "Let me think it over and talk with my husband." Then we—
Brazul', Vygranov, and I—left.

Document 51: Arnold Margolin Disputes
the Testimony of Vera Cheberiak

*Arnold D. Margolin testified that he had agreed to meet Cheberiak
when both were in Kharkov. But he categorically denied offering her
40,000 rubles to assume responsibility for the murder.*

Source: *Delo Beilisa: Stenograficheskii otchet.* Volume 1. Kiev, 1913.
Pp. 521–523 and 528–529.

MARGOLIN: I remember that Brazul' approached me some time in
November to meet Cheberiak. At the time there was persistent talk
that this woman knew everything and was considered an important
witness concerning the matter.... At the end of November Brazul'
observed that Cheberiak was complaining about the investigator. At first the investigator was affable toward her ... but for some
reason she had a wild look in her eyes.... Due to my experience
with criminal matters, Brazul' asked me to talk with her so I could
help him approach the case.... Brazul' informed me that Cheberiak wanted to reveal what she knew about the murder.... but she
would have to go to Kharkov to get additional information from
some thieves.... I then told Brazul' that I was planning to go to
Kharkov on business for a few days and that I'd meet with Cheberiak incognito if he could arrange to bring her to my hotel room....
I remember it like it was today. I left Kiev on the evening of December 6th and arrived in Kharkov the next morning.... Sometime

in the evening I received a phone call from Brazul', informing me
that he was in Kharkov and that he was ready to come over with
Cheberiak and a third person. I must say that he did not tell me
that the person was Vygranov. He only said that this person knew
everything and that I should not be shy in front of him. . . . And so
the three of them—Cheberiak, Brazul', and Vygranov—came to
my hotel. . . . She began by telling me that she had come to Kharkov
with only one purpose in mind: she wanted to get revenge against
Miffle, who had poisoned her children, recently viciously beat her,
and was the source of everything evil in her life. Right after this she
then disclosed that the murder took place in a cave a short distance
from the cave where the body was found, and that participating in
the homicide were Prikhodko,[1] Nezhinskaia,[2] Miffle. . . . As to the
motive, she stated that the boy Iushchinskii had known about the
family's criminal activities. And so his mother and step-father and
Miffle . . . realized that he had to be gotten rid of. . . . At the end of
our conversation Brazul' said to Cheberiak, "You are here because
you wanted to see someone in order to get more information." I
said that they should come see me the following day. And so the
next morning Brazul', Vygranov, and Cheberiak again came to my
hotel room. This time the conversation was very short since it became clear very quickly that Cheberiak was repeating what she had
said the evening before. I let Brazul' know that I considered further
meetings superfluous, cut off the conversation, and they left me. . . .
At that point I was in possession of the following facts: From the
very beginning Cheberiak slandered the relatives, beginning with
the mother, then the step-father, the uncle, and finally, Miffle. From
the moment of Beilis' arrest she began to calm down and became
completely quiet. And her behavior changed again during the second half of November when she found out from Brazul' that the
investigator had interrogated Malitskaia. It is evident that this story
about the investigator beginning to look like a wild animal started
after Malitskaia's testimony. Then the trip to Kharkov, her behavior,
her stories, her slandering of others . . . convinced me . . . that Cheberiak is not a witness, but a person involved in the murder in some
fashion. . . .

VIPPER: When you talked with Cheberiak, did you propose to her that if she were to take responsibility for the murder she would receive 40,000 rubles?

MARGOLIN: I think that this could have been proposed only by a lunatic.

SHMAKOV: Let me repeat: did you or did you not make that offer?

MARGOLIN: I answer as I did before: no. And there is nothing to call into question my mental capabilities.

SHMAKOV: So you did not propose to give her 40,000 rubles?

MARGOLIN: I already announced to the court that nothing was said about money.

1. Luka Prikhodko was Andrei's stepfather.
2. Natalia Nezhinskaia was Andrei's aunt.

Document 52: Nikolai Krasovskii Testifies on Behalf of Beilis

At the trial detective Nikolai A. Krasovskii testified about the evidence he had amassed during his investigation of the murder. He believed that Andrei had given the gang information about his school, which it planned to rob.

Delo Beilisa: Stenograficheskii otchet. Volume 1. Kiev, 1913. Pp. 547–553 and 564.

KRASOVSKII: I considered my dismissal unjust, especially since I had served with merit.

BOLDYREV: Thus, you believe that they dismissed you without cause?

KRASOVSKII: Yes, it was undeserved. Since I felt I was made to suffer on account of the Iushchinskii case, I set myself the goal of rehabilitating myself. . . . I didn't let Cheberiak from my sight. . . . The initial testimony of Shakhovskii . . . established that Zhenia Cheberiak, Andriusha Iushchinskii, and a third boy went off to play in Zagorovshchina, the area where the cave is located. It was here that Zhenia Cheberiak and Andriusha Iuschinskii got hold of some switches. Andrei's switch was longer and more flexible than Zhenia Cheberiak's switch. . . . Zhenia began to demand that Andriusha give him his switch. Andriusha refused and a quarrel took place. Zhenia declared, "If you do not give me the switch, I am going to tell your aunt that you are came here to hang out rather than go to school." And Andriusha replied, "If you tell this, then I will write to the police detectives that thieves hide out at your mother's and bring stolen goods there." Zhenia then went home and told his mother about the conversation. . . . I wanted to find out which people visited her. In order to ascertain this in detail, it was necessary to come into contact with those people who were close acquaintances with Cheberiak and who were well informed about Cheberiak's lifestyle. As a result I made the acquaintance of the Diakonova sisters. They constantly visited Cheberiak, and the entire gang of thieves spent time at Cheberiak's in the presence of the Diakonova sisters. The Diakonovas were welcomed by Cheberiak and they considered her a good friend. . . . On the fourteenth . . . Ekaterina Diakonova and Cheberiak went to sleep in the bed of Cheberiak's husband. Diakonova said that she didn't get undressed completely and only took off her boots and outer dress. She didn't fall asleep for a long time. When she had gone into the room she saw some kind of package in the corner. She asked Cheberiak what it was and Cheberiak said that it was stolen clothing. Then when Diakonova went to sleep and stretched her legs through the railing of the bed she touched the package, which felt dense, nothing like clothing. This was on the evening of the fourteenth. Early in August 1911 the Cheberiak children became sick. At this time Cheberiak was under arrest and the illness of her children coincided with her detention. . . . Cheberiak's husband said that. . . . it was a stomach ailment. Then Zhenia's leg began to swell up. . . . I advised the father to take the children to the hospital immediately. . . . It was clearly visible on the x-ray that there was part of a thorn in the heel. . . . On August 5 I received an order from the prosecutor to free Cheberiak. . . . She went to the hospital and took the boy home against the advice of the staff, even though his condition was grave and he was in agony. . . . Within two days Zhenia died. This turn of events struck me as suspicious, and so I instructed my assistants Vygranov and Polishchuk to keep constant watch on Cheberiak's apartment. I had in mind that Zhenia, who was often delirious, might say something. But his condition was so grave that he rarely regained consciousness. At those times when he did regain consciousness Cheberiak kept telling him: "Tell them, my dear boy, that your mother had nothing to do with it." Zhenia was in no condition to answer; he could only say, "Leave me alone, mama." He screamed in agony, "Andriusha, don't scream, don't scream." . . . When Zhenia began to say all this, his mother bent over and smothered him with kisses. He soon died. The other daughter was also gravely ill. . . . It turned out that Vera Cheberiak paid almost no attention to Valia during her illness . . . and forgot about her existence. . . . Cheberiak did not give her medicine . . . and there were times when . . . she locked the door of Valia's[1] room and left her and Liuda for the whole day while she was socializing with her friend Adel' Ravich. . . .

VIPPER: What did you think Cheberiak's connection to the Iushchin-skii murder was? You suggested that perhaps she was involved in the murder in order to provoke a pogrom?

KRASOVKSII: Yes, she was a participant in the murder.

VIPPER: In order to provoke a pogrom?

KRASOVSKII: Properly speaking there was one aim. To get rid of a dangerous witness who was in the gang and knew a great deal about the gang's present and past activities. The rumors about the murder having been committed by Jews came from her, which I saw as a maneuver to mislead the authorities.

VIPPER: In other words, there were two aims—one, to get rid of the boy who knew the gang's secrets, and two, to stimulate a pogrom.

KRASOVSKII: Yes.

1. Valia, or Valentina, was the youngest of the three Cheberiak children.

Document 53: The Testimony of Father Justin Pranaitis

The cross-examination of Father Justin Pranaitis, a Catholic priest, revealed his lack of knowledge about Judaism and discredited him as an expert witness for the prosecution.

Source: *Delo Beilisa: Stenograficheskii otchet.* Volume 3. Kiev, 1913. Pp. 434–435.

KARABCHEVSKII: As an expert, you drew conclusions based on sources. In your testimony I think you mentioned the tractate *Hullin.* What does *Hullin* mean?[1]

PRANAITIS: I don't know.

KARABCHEVSKII: So you do not remember your own expert testimony?

PRANAITIS: I cannot remember when I have read something.

KARABCHEVSKII: But you do know the tractate *Hullin*? What is its meaning?

PRANAITIS is silent.

KARABCHEVSKII: You are not able to tell us?

PRANAITIS is silent.

KARABCHEVSKII; What about the *Makhshirin*?[2] What does it mean?

PRANAITIS: This is outrageous. Why are you giving me a test?

KARABCHEVSKII: I am not. I want to have the meaning of the words clarified for myself because you have brought up Hebrew names.

SHMAKOV: The defense is examining the witness. This is not allowed.

BOLDYREV: The defense is interested in the translation of these words and has the right to ask the expert witness about this matter.

SHMAKOV: Perhaps it is proper to ask detailed questions. But he cannot remember. This is an examination.

BOLDYREV: The expert witness is a knowledgeable person, and he should not be tested.

SHMAKOV: He cannot remember every tractate.

KARABCHEVSKII: If it doesn't please Mr. Shmakov that I ask the expert witness Pranaitis these questions, I will not do so.

ZARUDNYI: But I consider myself to have the right to ask the expert witness about translations of words he refers to, and I have the right to know the meaning of these tractates. By the way, did you refer to the tractate *Yevamot*?[3]

PRANAITIS: I will not answer.

BOLDYREV: If the expert does not wish to answer, then it is prohibited to ask him.

ZARUDNYI: I will obey....

PRANAITIS is silent.

ZARUDNYI: And the tractate *She'elot U'Teshuvot*?[4]

PRANAITIS is silent.

ZARUDNYI: I want to place in the record that the expert witness answered that he did not know the meaning of the names of tractates that he refers to.

BOLDYREV: He announced that he did not want to answer.

ZARUDNYI: No, he answered that he does not know. But if he knows, then let him translate.

BOLDYREV: He is not obligated to do so.

ZARUDNYI: I asked him with your permission and request to place in the record that I did not give him an examination. But I asked him a question and received the answer that he does not know the meaning of the following tractates: *Yevamot*... and *She'elot U'Teshuvot*. I want the record to reflect that he refused to translate the names of the following tractates.

SHMAKOV to Zarudyni: Even you cannot read them.

ZARUDNYI: And so that's why I asked the expert witness because I cannot read Hebrew.

1. A tractate is a book of the Talmud. The tractate *Hullin* refers to the slaughter of animals and dietary laws.

2. The tractate of the Talmud that discusses foods and ritual impurity.

3. The tractate that refers to the mandated marriage of a widow to her brother-in-law.

4. *She'elot U'Teshuvot* is a compendium of responses or rabbinical correspondence on religious questions.

Document 54: Ivan Sikorskii Defends the Ritual Murder Accusation

The prosecution relied on the testimony of the eminent psychiatry professor Ivan Sikorskii, who claimed that the murder of Andrei had the hallmarks of a ritual killing. Unlike his statement from 1911 Sikorskii's comments at the trial explicitly accused Jews of ritual murder.

Source: *Delo Beilisa: Stenograficheskii otchet.* Volume 2. Kiev, 1913. Pp. 255–256.

SIKORSKII: The Jews are a nation of people who have talent for collecting information and detective work.... We can say with certainty that these murders (of Christian children) will not cease while there is ... agitation by races that nourish savagery among their members and while we are unable to take measures to liberate ourselves from them. They keep all this hush-hush, concealed, and secret—they think the child will be forgotten. But there are times when a child disappears and is then found stabbed to death and drained of blood. Then a special kind of hullabaloo begins. At first they direct suspicion toward relatives, then toward other Russians and Christians in general, . . . Both domestic and foreign Jews participate in this excitement.

KARABCHEVSKII: I humbly request that our protest against this testimony be placed on record.

GRIGOROVICH-BARSKII: We all protest! . . .

VIPPER: I ask the witness to base his views on the basis of psychiatry and psychology. Is this information known to you as an academic or is this your personal point of view?

SIKORSKII: My views are based on verified information. . . . The biggest misfortune for Jews is that fact that wealthy Jewish bankers are involved in concealing the commission of crimes. These capitalists hurl whatever they can to persecute their accusers. Whoever wants to struggle against this evil must do so with tremendous financial means. . . . Talmudism, Jewish capital and the Jewish press are all armed to fight together against their accusers.

4. SUMMATION AND VERDICT

Document 55: Grigorii Zamyslovskii Sums Up the Case against Beilis

Grigorii Zamyslovskii, who served as one of the civil plaintiffs, used the summation to reiterate the prosecution's insistence that Andrei was a victim of a ritual murder. He also challenged the contention of the defense that the murder occurred at the Cheberiak apartment and brushed aside weaknesses in the prosecution's case.

Source: *Delo Beilisa: Stenograficheskii otchet.* Volume 3. Kiev, 1913. Pp. 71–72, 74, 78–79, 86, and 90–91.

Let's return to the Cheberiak version for the final time. The accusation against her has been disproved and nothing remains of it. Eight witnesses were called to support the accusation. . . . But it is clear, you know, that the accusation is a total fabrication that tears apart at the seams. In addition, this version makes no sense for the following logical reasons. First, there was absolutely no motive. There was no cause or sense to the murder. For this version to make sense, we have to accept the slander that . . . Andriusha frequently spent the night at the Cheberiaks' and that he knew about the thieves' affairs. . . . Even if we consider that the thieves killed him out of fear that he gave them up, it is difficult to believe this version as credible. . . . Andriusha was almost never at the Cheberiaks. He moved to Slobodka a year before his death and he went to Lukianovka very rarely. What could he have seen? What could he have known? Why was he killed? . . . It is also unlikely that Singaevskii and Rudzinskii killed him. . . . On March 12th they robbed a store and immediately left for Moscow, where they were arrested for painting the town red. . . . I ask you how they could leave Cheberiak with the unburied body and go to Moscow at a time when . . . a search of Cheberiak's apartment was expected? . . . You remember that Cheberiak's apartment was located on the second floor, and a wine store was below it. Its windows looked over the yard where there were always people. . . . Does it make sense to kill someone under these circumstances? This is utterly unthinkable.

Prior to the murder the boy was seen between the brick factory and Cheberiak's apartment. . . . If he was not slaughtered at Cheberiak's, then where was he slaughtered? It had to be at the factory. . . . The tracks of Iushchinskii . . . lead to the factory. . . . Doesn't it make sense to conclude with full certainty based on the facts and not fantasy . . . that the murder occurred at the factory? . . .

Now we have firmly established that prior to the murder Iushchinskii was near the factory grounds . . . at the part of the factory where Mendel Beilis is boss. How do we know he went to the factory? We have the testimony of Shakhovskii, who heard it from Zhenia, that they had gone to ride on the clay grinder, where someone with a black beard . . . scared them off. Is there any reason not to believe Shakhovskii? . . . the direct testimony of the witness tells us that Iushchinskii went to the factory, and nothing refutes it. . . .

The murderers conceived and drew up a plan for murder ahead of time. According to the plan, the children had to go to the clay grinder. . . . But the children could have gone or not gone to the clay grinder, and so how could . . . this undertaking be left to chance? This only seems to be a contradiction.

Let's next look at the neck wounds. These are the wounds inflicted to drain blood. . . . Blood has immense significance for Jews. The soul of the body is in the blood. And where does the soul exit the body? From the same places where blood flows. It means, according to Jewish belief, that it comes from the neck. When they slaughter cattle, they cut the neck. This is the spot from which Jews draw blood.

In Russia, in 1817, the Emperor Alexander I issued an imperial decree that Jews are not to be persecuted for ritual murder without proof. . . . However, this does not mean that Emperor Alexander I rejected the existence of ritual murders. He only said that . . . Jews cannot be persecuted without proof. . . . In this case the savage murder occurred at the Zaitsev factory and Beilis was undoubtedly involved in the murder, which was done for ritual purposes. . . . Gentlemen of the jury, I am speaking on behalf of Alexandra Iushchinskaia[1] . . . But she is not the only one waiting for your verdict. All of Russia is waiting for your verdict.

1. Andrei's mother, who went by the last name of her second husband, Prikhodko.

Document 56: Chief Prosecutor Sums Up the Government's Case

Oskar Vipper took five hours to summarize the case for the jury. He used the time to accuse leaders of the Jewish community in Kiev of obstructing justice and using its grip on society and control of the press to divert police attention away from the guilty party, Beilis. His comments indicate that the prosecution was intent on countering accusations regarding the guilt of Vera Cheberiak.

Source: *Delo Beilisa: Stenograficheskii otchet.* Volume 3. Kiev, 1913. Pp. 4–5, 8, 17–18, 55, and 57–58.

It is sufficient to recall the famous trial of Dreyfus, it is sufficient to recall how it gave rise to world concern because one man, a Jew, was accused of high treason. And now only because a Jew is accused of such a bloody and savage crime, the world ought to be alarmed. I don't deny that it may be unpleasant and difficult for Jews that one of their tribe is on trial. I don't deny that it may be hard for him. . . .

From the very moment . . . that the stabbed body of Andriusha Iushchinskii was found, from that very moment . . . Jews took action to confuse and obscure the matter. . . . They tried to use all means to lead the investigating authorities away from the truth. . . .

The Jews suggested different versions: at first they accused relatives, then thieves, then again relatives, and yet again thieves. . . . Nevertheless, we are led to the Zaitsev factory, where the crime took place.

As the prosecutor, my task is not only to prove the guilt of the defendant, Beilis. My job is much more substantial. I have to prove that those persons . . . who have been called suspects and even accused of murder in the newspapers, are not guilty. Only after I have cleared them of these accusations . . . can I turn to my case against Beilis. . . .

The investigation was assigned to the chief of the investigative branch of the police, Mishchuk. . . . Mr. Mishchuk was an ideologue, apparently a Judeophile who does not believe that ritual murder exists in the twentieth century, in this enlightened century of airplanes and trams. . . .

From the moment that Beilis was arrested, Jewish circles became agitated. They did not expect that the government, or more accurately the investigating authorities and the procuracy, would dare to arrest Jews. I insist they did not expect this. You ask me why I am emphasizing this, why I am insisting on it. Of course the Jews have it tough. . . . Nevertheless, I want to say openly at the risk of being judged—not by a court but by society before which I stand—that I personally feel myself under the power of Jews, under the power of Jewish thought, and under the power of the Jewish press.

You see, the Russian press only seems Russian, but in reality almost all the organs of the print media are in the hands of the Jews. I don't want to say anything against the Jews, but when you read Jewish newspapers . . . and speak against them, you elicit the rebuke that you are a Black Hundred, an obscurantist, or a reactionary, that you do not believe in progress. . . . The Jews have seized control of the levers of society to such an extent that no one would want to bring up such an accusation not only in Russia, but even in other countries. . . . They are correct: Jews control capital. Even though they lack legal rights, they are in fact masters of our world. In this respect the prophecy of the Bible has almost come true: their condition may be difficult, but we feel as if we are under their yoke. . . .

We can see from a whole series of other trials in which blood was collected for Kabbalistic[1] ends, that Jews use blood and use needles to drain it. I will not bring up these at the trial, . . . Father Pranaitis's investigation is verified by scientific sources.

Members of the jury, it is now time for you to convict Beilis. You should not blot out from your thoughts the image of the dead . . . boy Iushchinskii. Let Beilis be innocent for the Jewish people, for the whole world, . . . but for the Russian person the name Beilis will never be holy. . . . Members of the jury, if you remember the image of this tortured boy and if you remember this fanatic who committed this evil deed with his own hands . . . you should give him the sentence that he deserves. We will not be afraid of pronouncing this sentence. . . . Many fair-minded people will hear your guilty verdict with calm satisfaction. I would not be standing here if I were not deeply convinced of his guilt and the guilt of his accomplices. . . . I wish you only one thing, namely that God will help you in your judgment.

1. The Kabbalah is a body of esoteric and mystical teachings in Judaism.

Document 57: The Defense Asserts the Innocence of Beilis

Oskar Gruzenberg, chief defense attorney, used his summary statement to point out the weaknesses and inconsistencies of the government's case against his client.

Source: *Delo Beilisa: Stenograficheskii otchet.* Volume 3. Kiev, 1913. Pp. 157–158, 181, 189, and 193.

No one . . . that the defense called to testify and no one that the prosecution called to testify had a word of reproach or complaint about Beilis. . . . Beilis has sat before you as a defendant, and before that he sat in prison for two-and-a-half years, an exhausted and stressed out man. Here he is being judged based on criticism of the Bible and the *Zohar,*[1] a book that nine-tenths of Jews have not seen and have not heard about, and based on the testimony of a drunken woman, from Wolf-Woman who was brought to court after the police looked for her in various haunts. God knows . . . the entire world of thieves tried to find evidence against Beilis. Sirs, I am certain that after only several months . . . you will remark . . . that we heard from Wolf-Woman, from Shakhovskii, who changed his testimony seventeen times during the investigation and so many times before you here in this court, and on the basis of frequently senseless and completely groundless evidence that was disconnected, confused, and scattered....

I ask you, what is he guilty of? ... You heard, as the prosecutor and civil plaintiffs stated, that the chapel attached to the clinic required human blood for its consecration.[2] Here I am addressing the prosecutor and say to him, if you believe that the chapel needs Christian blood in order to be built, and if you believe that the chapel led to the sacrifice and suffering of an unfortunate boy, then why are you silent and why don't you act upon your conviction? Search for the person who built the chapel.... You have seen this man, he has stood before you. He is Zaitsev, the son of the elder Zaitsev, the millionaire, who built the chapel. If the accuser believes that the chapel required Christian blood, then I ask you, why isn't he sitting here, the builder of this chapel, why aren't those who donated money to build the chapel sitting here ... and questioned about all this?.... Yes, I say to you that if you believe this, then you ought to charge them.... But you have not done so because you know very well that there is no evidence....

If this were some kind of ritual, some kind of religious ceremony, is it possible that they would take a dirty pillowcase with traces of semen and use this dirty pillowcase in a religious ritual ... in which the body was bathed in the presence of rabbis who recited prayers?....

You can destroy Beilis—this is within your authority. But you do not have the power to disgrace the Jewish religion. Forgive me, I do not mean to be impertinent, but what would it matter if you, who are entirely ignorant of Jewish writings and the history of the Jewish religion, should say that this religion condones the use of human blood? You would only add another groundless allegation, having no importance for anyone and coming besides from people who are entirely ignorant in these matters.

The Jewish religion is an ancient anvil, and its enemies have broken many sturdy hammers on it. But it has emerged pure, honest, and stoic from these trials....

The death of a person is dreadful, but even more dreadful is the possibility of accusations such as these occurring here—under the canopy of reason, conscience, and law.

1. The *Zohar* is a collection of books that include commentary on the Torah and form the basis of Jewish mystical thought. It first appeared in thirteenth-century Spain.

2. The owners of the brick factory had built a hospital and a small synagogue on its premises.

Document 58: Vasilii Maklakov Accuses
Vera Cheberiak of Andrei's Murder

Another defense attorney, Vasilii A. Maklakov, ridiculed the prosecution's case and accused Cheberiak of instructing her husband and daughter to perjure themselves.

Source: *Delo Beilisa: Stenograficheskii otchet.* Volume 3. Kiev, 1913. Pp. 126, 128–130, 145, and 153–155.

All evidence against Beilis is based on the testimony of Cheberiak. Once you stop believing Cheberiak, there will be no evidence against Beilis.

When I think about the actions of Brazul'-Brushkovskii and those who worked with him, gentlemen of the jury, I am simply offended and pained. It pains me to think that they were so naïve and simpleminded. . . . They thought that they would outwit Vera Cheberiak, they thought that she would help them get to the truth, but instead she led them by the nose. Take the trip to Kharkov. . . . Margolin and Brazul'-Brushkovskii did not understand what a dangerous game they were playing . . . and their honor depended on her. . . . If Cheberiak were to say here in court, "They summoned me to Kharkov and gave me 40,000 rubles in order to keep quiet about Beilis," what then? Perhaps it would be believable. The more someone knows something, the more money the person is given to be silent. If Cheberiak were to say in court, "they gave me 40,000 so I would testify against Miffle," again, this would not surprise me very much. . . . But when Cheberiak says that they gave her the money to take the blame for the murder of Iushchinskii, I say . . . who would offer 40,000 so she would admit in court that she killed Iushchinskii? . . . . What lawyers would be able to defend the murderer of Iushchinskii? Who would be able to say, "Yes, she murdered him, but let's take pity on her." . . .

What has transpired in this case is, frankly, bewildering. Cheberiak has been under suspicion right from the start, she has been jailed numerous times, but the investigating officials kept releasing her. Instead of holding onto that thread in order to unravel the tangled skein, instead of keeping her under close surveillance and monitoring her every move, she was led to believe that she was immune from prosecution. Why? Because the authorities were inclined to pursue other leads, to move in a different direction.

Why is Beilis on trial? We have been told that there was a plan to lure the boy Andriusha to the Zaitsev factory at an appointed time for a sacrifice. . . . According to the testimony of Cheberiak, supposedly based on what Zhenia and her little daughter told her, . . . a group of children that included Andriusha went to the brick factory to ride on the clay grinder. Beilis grabbed Andriushua in front of everyone and dragged him toward the kiln. All the others ran away, but Andriusha remained behind. I think the prosecution itself feels that this scenario is inconceivable. If you were to say that some villain killed Andriusha in a fit of savagery, . . . I could accept the story. But the children came to clay grinder, were grabbed, and destroyed. . . . It turns out that in order to conduct the sacrifice, they had to wait for that moment when a group of children decided to play on the clay grinder. If Andriusha had not gone to play then, the *tsaddiks* would be without a child to sacrifice and the chapel would not be consecrated. . . . if Beilis grabbed Andriusha and dragged him toward the kiln in view of our children . . . the whole neighborhood would have known once the children told their parents. . . . Cheberiak made up the story.

I ask myself, how did this come about? I cannot let myself think that those evil feelings, those unkind feelings that the prosecution in the course of two days awoke in you, that those feelings against the Jews have played a role in all of this. I will not believe this. I would not have known how to explain the accusation against Beilis if the prosecutor himself in his speech did not give me an answer, and if the private attorney did not add to what the prosecutor said. I am glad that they spoke straightforwardly because I can now provide an answer . . . without concealing anything.

You were told that this case was unique, and that it does not revolve around the unfortunate clerk named Beilis . . . but around the worldwide Jewish community. . . . Let's remember the words of the prosecutor, let's remember what he said about the Jews. . . . "The Jews did not expect the investigating authorities and the prosecutor to be bold enough to bring charges." . . .

Behind Beilis's back some kind of strange struggle was playing out. . . . And this was a misfortune for justice. If we want a just sentence, then all of us must serve justice, all of us, starting with the defense and prosecution and ending with our judges, should say to you: don't repeat this mistake, gentlemen of the jury, be heroic, rise above these fears, and understand that all our mistakes, all the mistakes of Jewish bosses and all the mistakes committed by the Jewish people have nothing to do with how you judge Beilis. . . .

They have said to you that the Jews are our enemies, that they scorn us, that they do not consider us people. . . . Resist, gentlemen of the jury, because if you judge Beilis independently of the evidence, but judge him for our sins, . . . then he will be atoned, since, in the end, even if we were to find people who initially welcome your judgment, eventually they will understand it to be a sad page in the history of our judicial system. There will be people who at first will be glad about your sentence, but then they will see your verdict as a sad page in the history of our judicial system. Remember this when you decide the fate of Beilis, gentlemen of the jury.

Document 59: The Judge Instructs the Jury

Judge Boldyrev followed the indictment by dividing the charges into two questions, thereby allowing the jury to determine the guilt of Beilis separately from whether or not a ritual murder had occurred.

Source: DAKO, *fond* 863, *opis'* 10, *delo* 16, *listy* 422–423. Excerpted from the microfilm collection "Beilis Case Papers," copyright East View Information Services.

Has it been proved that on March 12, 1911, in the Jewish clinic in one of the buildings of the brick factory belonging to the merchant Mark Zaitsev, that . . . Andrei Iushchinskii was gagged and wounded by a pointed instrument in the parietal, occipital, and temporal lobes as well as on the neck with accompanying wounds to the cerebral vein, arteries of the left temple, and veins in the neck, resulting in abundant bleeding and then, after losing five glasses of blood, additional wounds were caused by the same implement to the torso, accompanied by wounds to the lungs, liver, right kidney, and the heart, and that these wounds, which totaled forty-seven, caused Iushchinskii agonizing pain and led to the almost complete loss of blood and to his death?

If the event described in the first question has been proved, then is the accused defendant . . . Menachim-Mendel Tevye Beilis, thirty-nine-years old, guilty of colluding in a premeditated plan with persons not yet discovered to deprive out of religious fanaticism the boy Andrei Iushchinskii, thirteen years old, of his life on March 12, 1911 . . . in the brick factory belonging to the merchant Mark Zaitsev, and did the accused defendant, in order to carry out his intentions, seize Iushchinskii whom he found there and carry him off to one of the buildings of the factory, where with the prior agreement of persons unknown with whom he agreed to deprive Iushchinskii of his life? Beilis gagged Iushchinskii and with a pointed implement wounded him in the parietal, occipital, and temporal lobes as well as on the neck with accompanying wounds to the cerebral vein, arteries of the left temple, and veins in the neck, resulting in abundant bleeding. And after losing five glasses of blood, did Iushchinskii receive additional wounds from the same implement to the torso, accompanied by wounds to the lungs, liver, right kidney, and the heart, and did these wounds, which totaled forty-seven, caused Iushchinskii agonizing pain and lead to the almost complete loss of blood and to his death?

Document 60: The Foreign Press Announces the Verdict

The foreign press followed closely the proceedings of the trial. Special correspondents sent daily reports to their editors and offered their obser-vations of the government's case, which they tended to characterize as based on flimsy if not bogus evidence. While they applauded the acquit-tal of Beilis, they were perturbed by the jury's decision to go along with the prosecution's assertion that Andrei's death was the result of ritual murder. The following two reports come from the Times of London.

Source: *The Times of London,* no. 40,366 (November 11, 1913): 8 and no. 40,367 (November 12, 1913): 9. Spelling has been changed for consistency.

November 11. An Ambiguous Verdict: The Kiev "ritual murder" trial ended yesterday in a verdict acquitting Beilis of the charge of having mur-dered the boy Iushchinskii, but declaring that the murder was committed in the brickyard or factory belonging to the well-known Jewish family Zaitsev.

While satisfactory in so far as it absolves Beilis of the monstrous charge preferred against him on the flimsiest of evidence, the verdict must be regarded as eminently calculated to perpetuate the agitation by which the trial has been accompanied. In fairness to the Russian jury, it must be noted that the questions formulated by the presiding Judge practically prescribed the verdict to be rendered. Its effect will be to remove the burden of the accusation from the shoulders of the unfortunate Beilis, who has been kept in prison since his arrest in August 1911, while casting suspicion on to the Jewish community as a whole. . . .

Not until supplementary details of the final proceedings have been received will it be advisable, or, indeed, possible, to pass judgment upon this latest revival of the ancient anti-Jewish legend; but we register with especial satisfaction the energetic disclaimer addressed to us by Professor J. G. Frazer—the well-known author of *The Golden Bough* and the foremost British authority on comparative mythology—of the construction placed upon a distorted passage from his work by a Russian journal the *Two-Headed Eagle*. We reproduced in our later editions yesterday the authentic text of this passage, which in itself refutes the conclusions drawn from it by the *Two-Headed Eagle,* and apparently also by other Russian journals of greater influence and repute.

November 12. For some reason or another, the Court asked the jury to determine a second point, besides that of the guilt of innocence of the accused. It asked them to say whether the murder was or was not committed in the Jewish factory owned by Zaitsev, in which Beilis was a foreman. They answered that it was, and they also accepted the contention of the prosecution that the murdered boy had been tortured, and that his body had been almost drained of blood. . . . The malicious and fanatical enemies of the Jews may represent the findings and regard them, it is to be feared, as amounting to a verdict that, although Beilis is innocent, a Jewish ritual murder has in fact been committed. . . . It is to be regretted that the issues put to the jury admitted of a reply which seems to countenance the most shocking part of the Crown case, and which will almost certainly be used by Russian reactionaries to perpetuate a horrible and malicious legend.

That this legend should find credence, not only amongst the ignorant and superstitious peasants, or amongst political and religious reactionaries who for their own purposes strongly wish to believe it, but also in the minds of intellectual and highly cultivated men, some of whom hold very "advanced" opinions on all spiritual matters, is the most astonishing and the most humiliating feature in the whole of this amazing trial. Yet our Correspondent assures us that this is the case. Thousands of Russians, he tells us, who burn with righteous indignation at the prosecution of Beilis because they see that there is no shred of real evidence against him, are firmly convinced that the Jews do practice ritual murder....

Document 61: Aleksei Shmakov Claims Victory

Notwithstanding the acquittal of Beilis, defenders of the government's case asserted that the prosecution had won the case because the jury supported the claim of ritual murder.

Source: *Vecherniaia gazeta* (The Evening Gazette), no. 162 (October 29, 1913): 1.

We have no intention of reversing the sentence of the court because the sentence satisfies us. It was necessary for us to establish that the murder had a ritual character, and we were able to do so. The jurors knew that the crime was carried out at Zaitsev's factory, that the murder was accompanied by... wounds of a ritual nature, that the murder was carried out with the aim of obtaining blood, of which the murderers collected five glasses, and it is evident from the order and wording of the questions that it was a ritual "murder," even though the word was not used in the charge to the jurors.

Had the jury said that the prosecution had not proven the ritual aspect of the murder, we would not have been satisfied, even if the jurors had found Beilis guilty of murder.

Document 62: The Antisemitic Press Defends the Prosecution

As one mouthpiece for antisemites in Kiev, Dvuglavyi orel (The Double-Headed Eagle) maintained that the verdict vindicated its position that Andrei had been the victim of a ritual murder carried out by Jews.

Source: *Dvuglavyi orel* (The Double-Headed Eagle), no. 44 (October 30, 1913): 1.

It's over. The court has acquitted Beilis. But the court has accused all kikes for using Christian blood. The kikes exult . . . in the acquittal of Beilis. The kikes ignore the circumstance, you see, that the murder of Andriusha was a ritual killing, carried out with the aim of using Christian blood. I don't know whether the kikes would have preferred the acquittal of Beilis or to have him cast under the shadow of guilt for all time. The torturers of Christian children exult, but their criminality has been proven with exhaustive clarity in court.

EPILOGUE

Document 63: Beilis Returns Home

In his memoirs Beilis described his release from prison after his acquittal and the crowds of well-wishers who besieged his house, hoping to catch a glimpse of him and offer their congratulations.

Source: Mendel Beilis, *The Story of My Sufferings*. New York: Mendel Beilis Publishing Company, 1926. Pp. 199–200, 204, and 208–209.

The captain of the station was a notorious Black Hundred anti-Semite. He could not endure the sight of a Jew. . . . No sooner had I entered the police station than the captain came out with arms outstretched. "I am very happy to see you." He shook hands with me very cordially. "I want to ask a favor of you, Beilis, and I hope you won't refuse me."

"What can I do for you?"

"My daughter wishes to see you. She wishes to congratulate you upon liberation. Will you permit her that pleasure? She is a Gymnasium student, who was terribly excited during the whole period of your trial. Every time she read the papers and saw that something had gone wrong with your affairs, she wept like a child. She neglected her studies because of you. She used to go around moaning: 'Oh, my God, how the poor man must be suffering.' Now you must permit her to come and greet you."

During the course of this speech the policemen at the station looked at their captain as though he were a madman. It was an unusual picture for them to see their savage captain imploring a Jew for a favor; it was usually the reverse. And the official apparently considered it an honor for his daughter to talk to me.

Of course, I was only too glad to grant him his request, and said that I myself would be pleased to meet his daughter. . . . While waiting for his daughter, he wanted to entertain me. "Would you like to drink something—tea or beer?" . . . Tea was brought in; the policeman who offered me the cup gave me the military salute.

The captain's daughter entered a few minutes later accompanied by a girlfriend. The two seemed quite bashful and hesitated to come over.

"Well," encouraged the captain, "Don't be shy. Greet your friend Beilis." The girl finally came over and asked very timidly: "Are you Mr. Beilis? You must forgive me for being so bold. Here is a friend of mine; we both used to pray for you and weep for your liberation." . . .

"We suffered so much because of you," said the girl. "We did not sleep whole nights; and always talked of your sufferings, but of course it was nothing compared to what you have gone through. But now, justice and truth have won out. I wish you peace and happiness together with your family." . . .

I believed that once freed, I would enjoy my former quiet life in the house. It was not to be so, however. My house was daily besieged by people coming to greet me and to express their joy at my liberation. Not only individuals, but groups of fifty and sixty people would come to the house at one time. The cabmen at the railroad stations, seeing groups of Jews descending from the trains would straightway ask: "Are you going to Beilis?," and they would drive them straight to me.

Dozens of automobiles always stood in front of my house. One party would leave and another would come. People brought flowers, chocolates; everyone wished to bring me something. The house was turned into a flower garden and a candy shop.

The whole procedure gave me great moral satisfaction. I saw the world taking an immense interest in my tribulations, and coming to me in order to express their joy at my liberation. I was very thankful, of course, though I must admit that the continuous handshaking was anything but pleasant for my hands, which became swollen after a time. . . .

There were no less than seven or eight thousand visitors a day at my home. During the period immediately following the trial I received eleven thousand letters in all European languages, from all parts of the world, and seven thousand telegrams. Some of the telegrams were long messages; twenty-thousand visiting cards completed the collection. . . .

It was during this time that the rumor began circulating that I was receiving money from many sources. The truth is that some people sent me a few rubles on a few occasions, why, I don't know. But the papers had it that I was becoming a millionaire. The result was that I was deluged by hundreds of letters asking for financial aid. Talmud Torahs, rabbis, hospitals, charity institutions, and innumerable committees asked for money! Students appealed for money to see them through college. One Jew had to marry off his daughter, and therefore he demanded a dowry. . . . Nor were any of these requests for meager sums of hundreds of rubles. They went in for big money. No one asked for less than a few thousand. Meanwhile, the truth of the situation was that I needed help myself. I had not a cent left of my savings and did not know what the near future had in store for me. Among the numerous letters of sympathy that I received were also a number of messages from the Black Hundreds, threatening me with death. I could not, therefore, feel completely assured even of my safety.

Document 64: Beilis Leaves Russia

Fear for his own safety and that of his family, as well as the realization that his fame would not allow him to return to a normal family and working life, led Beilis to consider leaving Russia for a new life elsewhere.

Source: Mendel Beilis, *The Story of My Sufferings*. New York: Mendel Beilis Publishing Company, 1926. Pp. 210 and 214–215.

The threats addressed to me by the Black Hundreds multiplied. Each day brought its quota of ominous notes. In addition, the Governor of Kiev insisted that I leave the city, for he could not be responsible for my safety. My situation was a difficult one. If I could not remain in Kiev and retain my former position, I was deprived of all sources of income, and would be unable to support my family. Financial worries began. Instead of renewing my quiet life, as I had expected, I had to begin thinking of moving somewhere else, and of starting life anew. . . .

Then the committee wanted to know what occupation I would choose for myself. "We shall give you the means to take up whatever you like. Do not consider it as a gift. It is merely our duty to you."

I could hardly decide upon anything specific. It was all so definite and concrete. I had to say: "Gentlemen, I cannot decide upon anything just now. I believe that it would be best if you were to make up my mind for me. I would not be averse to having a little house which would bring sufficient income for a modest living, and a piece of land connected with it which I should be able to work. I like farming very much, and I always wanted to live on the land." . . .

The plan was to have me go to Trieste first and to get a month's rest there, and then embark for Palestine. I began preparing myself for a parting with Holy Russia. I must confess that it was not easy. There were many Black Hundreds in Russia who were eager to shed Jewish blood, but on the other hand there were so many wonderful Russians. How many Russian prisoners, supposedly depraved people, had wept with me in jail; how many Russian children had not slept nights and prayed to God for my release? And then the Russian intelligentsia, what an interest they had displayed in my case, how much energy they had spent for my sake, and how great was the joy of these people, when their efforts resulted in my liberation!

My impressions were obtained not only from the hundreds of Christians who had come to my house to greet me and to rejoice with me, but from the numerous letters I received and the indirect reports. In addition to harboring a fondness for these people, it was difficult to part with my native land, where I had been born, grown up, had suffered, and enjoyed life.

It was planned that my departure was to be kept a secret. No one, not even my relatives, were to know. We had to take these various precautions because my life was in danger. . . .

My departure occurred in December 1913, and although we believed it had been kept a secret, events showed that it had not. In a few days after I had secured my passport, the newspapers had big headlines that I was to go abroad. We were not very anxious to have the anti-Semites know that I proposed leaving Russia. But since the day and hour of my departure was not known, I was safe. . . .

Notes

Introduction: A Murder without a Mystery

1. Until February 1918 Russia used the Julian calendar, which in the twentieth century was thirteen days behind the Gregorian calendar used in the rest of the Western world. All dates are given according to the Julian calendar.

2. Hasidim are adherents of a branch of Orthodox Judaism that emerged in the eighteenth century in Eastern Europe. Hasidism focuses on the spiritual and mystical aspects of Judaism and challenges traditional Judaism's emphasis on the study of texts. Hasidism is comprised of family dynasties established by charismatic leaders.

3. The administration of the library refused to hand over the collection, and later in 1992 the Russian government nullified the court's decision. The books have remained in legal limbo since the early 1990s: as recently as 2010 a judge in Washington, D.C., ruled that Lubavitchers are the rightful owners of the library, but the Russian Ministry of Foreign Affairs rejected the decision. To date, the Lenin Library has transferred only 30 books to Lubavitchers, all of which are duplicates of books already in Brooklyn. For a summary of these events, see Konstantin Akinsha and Patricia Grimsted, "On the Way Back: The Schneerson Collection and the Return of the 'Smolensk Archive'," in Ekaterina Genieva, Patricia Kennedy Grimsted, Karina Dmitrieva, and Mariana Tax Choldin, eds., *The Return of the "Smolensk Archive,"* 232–271; Sherry Hutt and David Tarler, eds., *Yearbook of Cultural Property Law 2010*; and Michael Bazyler and Seth Gerber, "Chabad v. Russian Federation: A Case Study in the Use of American Courts to Recover Looted Cultural Property," *International Journal of Cultural Property* 17 (2010): 361–386.

4. Some general works on ritual murder are Alan Dundes, ed., *The Blood Libel Legend*; Jonathan Frankel, *The Damascus Affair: "Ritual Murder," Politics, and the Jews in 1840*; R. Po-Chia Hsia, *The Myth of Ritual Murder: Jews and Magic in Reformation Germany*; Gavin Langmuir, *Toward a Definition of Antisemitism*; and Joshua Trachtenberg, *The Devil and the Jews: The Medieval Conception of the Jew and Its Relation to Modern Antisemitism*.

5. Helmut Walser Smith, *The Butcher's Tale: Murder and Anti-Semitism in a German Town*, 97; Gavin Langmuir, *Toward a Definition of Antisemitism*, 263–281.

6. The *strappado* is a form of torture in which the victim's hands are tied behind her or his back. The victim is lifted into the air by a rope that is attached to the wrists. In order to intensify what must already be excruciating pain, weights may added to the feet. Once the victim is suspended in the air, the rope is loosened, thereby dropping the victim partway to the ground. *Strappado* also refers to the device that carries out the torture.

7. R. Po-Chia Hsia, *Trent 1475: Stories of a Ritual Murder Trial*.

8. Helmut Walser Smith notes that Protestants in German-speaking Europe tended to reject the ritual murder charge over time, while "the idea of ritual murder retained more of a hold" on Catholics. See *The Butcher's Tale*, 107.

9. Paweł Maciejko, "Christian Accusations of Jewish Human Sacrifice in Early Modern Poland: The Case of Jan Serafnowicz," *Gal-Ed* 22 (2010): 15–66; Zenon Guldon and Jacek Wijaczka, *Procesy o mordy rytualne w Polsce w XVI–XVIII wieku*; Hanna Węgrzynek, *"Czarna legenda" Żydów: Procesy o rzekome mordy rytualne w dawney Polsce*; Daniel Tollet, *Accuser pour convertir: du bon usage de l'accusation de crime ritual dans la Pologne catholique à l'époque modern*; Šiaučiūnaitė-Verbickienė, "Blood Libel in a Multi-Confessional Society: The Case of the Grand Duchy of Lithuania," *East European Jewish Affairs* 38, no. 2 (2008): 201–209; and Jacek Wijaczka, "Ritual Murder Accusations in Poland Throughout the 16th to 18th Centuries," in Susanna Buttaroni and Stanisław Musiał, eds., *Ritual Murder: Legend in European History*, 195–209.

10. Magda Teter, *Sinners on Trial: Jews and Sacrilege after the Reformation*, 183 and 209–210.

11. Walser Smith, *The Butcher's Tale*, 123.

12. Robert Rockaway and Arnon Gutfeld, "Demonic Images of the Jew in the Nineteenth Century United States," *American Jewish History* 89, no. 4 (2002): 355–381.

13. I am not the first to stress this point. For a similar argument, see Jacob Katz, *From Prejudice to Destruction: Antisemitism, 1700–1933*.

14. Vasilii Rozanov in particular was obsessed with what he believed was the significance of blood for Jews. For a discussion of Rozanov's views on Jews, blood, and ritual murder, see Laura Engelstein, *The Keys to Happiness: Sex and the Search for Modernity in Fin-de-Siècle Russia*, 299–333.

15. Precise data are difficult to obtain. Estimates range from 500,000 to 1,000,000.

16. Uniates acknowledge papal authority and doctrine, but retain many Eastern Orthodox rites and rituals.

17. See John Klier, "The Origins of the 'Blood Libel' in Russia," *Newsletter of the Study Group on Eighteenth-Century Russia* 14 (1986): 12–22; and Robert Weinberg, "Look! Up There in the Sky: It's a Vulture, It's a Bat . . . It's a Jew," in Eugene Avrutin and Harriet Murav, eds., *Jews in the East European Borderlands*, 167–186.

18. Udmurts live in a region of the Ural Mountains, some 800 miles east of Moscow.

19. The author of this study was Vladimir I. Dal', a linguist who compiled a comprehensive dictionary of the Russian language.

20. John Klier, *Imperial Russia's Jewish Question, 1855–1881*, 417–436.

21. See the essays in John Klier and Shlomo Lambrozo, eds., *Pogroms: Anti-Jewish Violence in Modern Russian History.*

22. Charles Ruud and Sergei Stepanov, *Fontanka 16: The Tsar's Secret Police*, 246–273.

23. Arnold Margolin, *The Jews of Eastern Europe*, 163.

24. Ibid., 167.

25. In 1840 a group of Jews in Damascus were accused of killing a Capuchin friar for religious purposes. Torture elicited confessions of guilt, but a delegation of prominent European Jews prevailed upon Muhammad Ali of Egypt, ruler of Syria at the time, and secured their release. See Jonathan Frankel, *The Damascus Affair: "Ritual Murder," Politics, and the Jews in 1840.* Alfred Dreyfus was a captain in the French army falsely accused of selling military secrets to Germany. Convicted two times on fabricated evidence, Dreyfus spent five years in solitary confinement on Devil's Island before receiving a government pardon and being set free. See Ruth Harris, *Dreyfus: Politics, Emotion, and the Scandal of the Century.* Leo Frank was an American Jew convicted of killing a teenage girl who worked in the pencil factory he managed. A mob seized Frank while he was in jail and lynched him in 1915. He was pardoned in 1986. See Alfred Lindemann, *The Jew Accused: Three Anti-Semitic Affairs: Dreyfus, Beilis, Frank, 1894–1915.*

1. The Initial Investigation

1. Michael Hamm, *Kiev: A Portrait, 1800–1917*, 128; and Natan Meir, *Kiev, Jewish Metropolis: A History, 1859–1924*, 23–27.

2. The police also rounded up Jews living illegally in the city and expelled them.

According to historian Natan Meir, more than 1,000 Jewish families were expelled in 1910. Meir, *Kiev, Jewish Metropolis*, 129–130.

3. Faith Hillis, "Between Empire and Nation: Urban Politics, Community, and Violence in Kiev, 1863–1907," 498.

4. Hamm, *Kiev*, 201–203.

5. In August 1911 *Russkoe znamia* reported that a long strand of hair, apparently from a beard, had been found on Andrei's body. The paper asserted that the "composition of the hair indicates that it undoubtedly belongs to a Semitic person." Also noting that the hair came from an uncut beard, the paper concluded that since Hasidim do not trim their beards, the strand of hair belonged to a Jew. No. 176 (August 9, 1911): 2.

6. In a speech in November 1911 Zamyslovskii went so far as to insinuate that the murder could have occurred only with the assistance of the local police. Either the Jews had bribed the police to cover up the crime or the police cooperated in the commission of the murder. *Kievlianin*, no. 309 (November 8, 1911): 4.

7. Vasilii Shulgin, *The Years: Memoirs of a Member of the Russian Duma, 1906–1907,* 108–109. After the trial Shulgin faced charges for deliberately disseminating "false evidence" in an editorial that criticized the prosecution's conduct during the investigation of the murder. A jury found Shulgin guilty, but Tsar Nicholas II pardoned him.

8. Victoria Khiterer, "Vasilii Shul'gin and the Jewish Question: An Assessment of Shul'gin's Antisemitism," *On the Jewish Street: A Journal of Russian-Jewish History and Culture* 1, no. 2 (2011): 146.

9. Andrei's biological father, whom his mother had not married, had abandoned his family early on and probably perished during the Russo-Japanese War in 1904–1905. The boy's grandmother conferred her married name, Iushchinskii, on him.

10. Krasovksii and others believed that Andrei either served as a lookout for the gang or had been approached by the gang to give it information about the church school he attended in preparation to rob it. It was also possible that Andrei was privy to the illegal activities of Cheberiak simply by the fact that he frequented the house and played with Zhenia.

11. The blood may have been Andrei's, and the semen stains probably resulted from the orgies rumored to have occurred in the apartment.

12. *Delo Beilisa: Stenograficheskii otchet,* vol. 1, 643–644.

13. It is also possible that Diakonova believed that Andrei's spirit, and not his physical body, was present in the room.

14. The historian Sergei Stepanov raised the possibility that a sexual predator may have killed Andrei, but he did not offer compelling evidence. Also, the two autopsy reports found no evidence of sexual abuse. Sergei Stepanov, *Chernaia sotnia v Rossii, 1905–1914 gg.,* 318–319.

2. The Case against Beilis

1. Sikorskii died in 1919. His son Igor, who emigrated to the United States in that year, was the aviation engineer who developed the helicopter.

2. This was the first time the full name of the bearded Jewish man known as Mendel appeared in police records.

3. Anna Zakharova went by the nickname "Wolf-Woman" because she slept outside in an area called the "wolf's ravine."

4. Rogger, "The Beilis Case: Anti-Semitism and Politics in the Reign of Nicholas II," 626.

5. Ibid., 625–626.

6. The gendarmes were a special branch of the police responsible for state security and other law enforcement duties.

7. Alexander Tager, *The Decay of Czarism: The Beilis Trial,* 52.

8. A documentary film based on the findings of Brazul'-Brushkovskii screened in August 1912 in a few cinemas in Russia and abroad.

9. *Peisakh* is the Yiddish word for Passover. Andriusha is an affectionate diminutive of Andrei.

3. The Trial

1. Vasilii Shulgin, *The Years: Memoirs of a Member of the Russian Duma, 1906–1917*, 111.

2. Alexander Afanas'ev, "Jurors and Jury Trials in Imperial Russia, 1866–1885," in Ben Eklof, John Bushnell, and Larissa Zakharova, eds., *Russia's Great Reforms, 1885–1881*, 219.

3. *Kievskaia mysl'*, no. 267 (September 27, 1913): 3.

4. Perhaps Shmakov and Zamyslovskii believed Andrei's mother was entitled to a monetary award based on Andrei's projected earnings or had suffered a loss of honor because her son's body was mutilated.

5. DAKO, *fond* 183, *opis'* 5, *delo, listy* 6, 8–8 *oborot*.

6. Maria Carlson, "Fashionable Occultism: Spiritualism, Theosophy, Freemasonry, and Hermeticism in Fin-de-Siècle Russia," in Bernice Glatzer Rosenthal, ed., *The Occult in Russian and Soviet Culture*, 138.

7. V. I. Fenenko deposed Archimandrite Ambrosius of Pochaevo-Uspenskaia Monastery in May 1911. The cleric stated that he lacked first-hand knowledge of ritual murder, noting that his testimony was based on what two monks, who had converted from Judaism, told him about the religious needs of Jews for Christian blood.

8. A translation of the pamphlet, *The Secret Rabbincal Teachings Concerning Christians*, can be found at www.romancatholicism.org.

9. Genrikh Reznik, Rafail Ganelin, Viktor E. Kel'ner, et al., *Delo Mendela Beilisa: Materialy Chrezvychoinoi sledstvennoi komissi Vremennogo pravitel'stava o sudebnom protsesse 1913 g. po obvineniiu v ritual'nom ubiistve*, 65–66.

10. According to one newspaper account, the police had gone to the small town of Lubavitch, where the head of the Schneersohn dynasty resided, to inquire whether "the witness Schneersohn in the Beilis case" was a relative. The woman who answered the door of the rebbe's house gave a resounding "No" as her response. *Kievskaia mysl'*, no. 24 (October 19, 1913).

11. DAKO, fond, 183, opis' 5, delo 4, listy 85–85 obratno. An article in *Zemshchina* proclaimed that the brick factory was a "Hasidic den" where Jews tried to hide their "fanatical Jewish souls" by wearing "fashionable European clothing." *Zemshchina*, no. 1473 (October 18, 1913), 2.

4. Summation and Verdict

1. The attorneys for Beilis tended to take two approaches in their closing statements: one focused on demonstrating Beilis's innocence, while the second debunked the ritual murder accusation. Nikolai Karabchevskii, however, pursued an alternative route, suggesting that the murder was part of an effort by the killers

to spark an anti-Jewish pogrom and thereby divert the attention of the police away from Vera Cheberiak and her gang.

2. Oskar Gruzenberg, *Yesterday: Memoirs of a Russian-Jewish Lawyer*, 107.

3. One newspaper reported that at the start of the trial most jurors believed Beilis was guilty and assumed the defense had bribed its witnesses. But as the trial went on more of the jurors became convinced of his innocence. They grew skeptical of the government's witnesses whose testimony, from their perspective, undermined the case against Beilis. Some jurors believed that Vera Cheberiak, at the very least, knew who murdered Andrei. *Kievskaia mysl'*, no. 250 (October 30, 1913): 3.

4. *Kievskaia mysl'*, no. 299 (October 29, 1913): 2; and no. 300 (October 30, 1913): 1.

5. *Vechernaia gazeta* no. 162 (October 29, 1913): 1. Even before the trial ended, Chaplinskii informed an editor at *Kievlianin* that the prosecution did not care if the jury found Beilis guilty. It was more important to support the government's allegation that a ritual murder had occurred. Jacob Lerner, "Corruption and the Counterrevolution: The Rise and Fall of the Black Hundreds," 137.

6. *Kievskaia mysl'*, no. 301 (October 31, 1913): 4.

Epilogue

1. Joel Berkowitz, "The 'Mendel Beilis Epidemic' on the Yiddish Stage," *Jewish Social Studies* 8, no. 1 (2010): 199–225. In 1917 a film entitled *Delo Beilisa* (The Beilis Affair) was released in Kiev.

2. http://der-stuermer.org/english/judical-inc.htm.

3. Tomasso Calio, "The Cult of the Alleged Ritual Murder Victims in the Second Half of the 20th Century in Italy," in Susanna Buttaroni and Stanisław Musiał, eds., *Ritual Murder: Legend in European History*, 225–245. In 1989 a Jewish woman with multiple personality disorder appeared on *The Oprah Winfrey Show* and told viewers that she had witnessed the ritual sacrifice of Jewish children by their parents. For an edited transcript of the interview, see http://usajewish.blogspot .com/2007/02/vicki-and-devil.html.

4. A brief description of the speech can be found at http://virtualjerusalem .com/news.php?Itemid=6621. Accessed April 18, 2012.

5. The *Protocols of the Elders of Zion* first appeared in Russian in the early years of the twentieth century and gained worldwide popularity by World War I. Translated into many languages, the *Protocols* has become the bible of antisemites. Today, textbooks in the Arab Middle East teach the book as the truth, and in 2002 Egyptian television aired a miniseries inspired by the *Protocols*. See Stephen Bronner, *A Rumor about the Jews: Reflections on Antisemitism and the Protocols of the Learned Elders of Zion* (New York, 2009); and Norman Cohn, *Warrant for Genocide: The Myth of the Jewish World Conspiracy and the Protocols of the Elders of the Zion* (New York: Harper and Row, 1967), for information on the *Protocols*.

Bibliography

Archives

Derzhavnyi arkiv Kyïvs'koi oblasti (Archive of the Kiev Region)

Newspapers

Dvuglavyi orel (The Double-Headed Eagle)
Evreiskie izvestiia (Jewish News)
Kievlianin (The Kievan)
Kievskaia mysl' (Kievan Thought)
Narodnaia kopeika (The People's Kopek)
Novoe vremia (New Times)
Russkaia znamia (The Russian Banner)
Vechernaia gazeta (The Evening Gazette)
Zemshchina (The Realm)

Document Collections

Danylenko, V. ed. *The Beilis Case Papers: Dokumenty po delu Beilisa.* 7 vols. Minneapolis: East View Information Services, 2005.
Delo Beilisa: Stenograficheskii otchet. 3 vols. Kiev: T-vo "Pechatnia S.P. Iakovleva," 1914.
Leikin, Ezekiel. *The Beilis Transcripts: The Anti-Semitic Trial that Shook the World.* Northvale, NJ: Jason Aronson, Inc., 1993.
Reznik, Genrikh, Viktor Kel'ner, Rafail Ganelin, et al. *Delo Mendelia Beilisa: Materialy Chrezvychainoi sledstvennoi komissii Vremennogo pravitel'stva o sudebnom protsesse 1913 g. po obvineniiu v ritual'nom ubiistve.* St. Petersburg: DB, 1999.
Shchegolev, P. E., ed. *Padenie tsarskogo rezhima: Stenograficheskie otchety doprosov i pokazanii dannykh v 1917 g. v Chrezvychainoi sledstvennoi komissi Vremennogo pravitel'stva.* 7 vols. Moscow-Leningrad, 1924–1927.

Articles and Books

Afanas'ev, Alexander. "Jurors and Jury Trials in Imperial Russia, 1866–1885." In *Russia's Great Reforms, 1855–1881,* Ben Eklof, John Bushnell, and Larissa Zakharova, eds. Bloomington: Indiana University Press, 1984.

Akinsha, Konstantin, and Patricia Grimsted. "On the Way Back: The Schneerson Collection and the Return of the 'Smolensk Archive'." In *The Return of the "Smolensk Archive,"* Patricia Grimsted, Karina Dmitrieva, and Mariana Tax Choldin, eds. Moscow: ROSSPEN, 2005.

Al'bom "Delo Beilisa" v risunkakh i fotografiiakh. Kiev: Petr Barski, 1913.

Bartoshevich, Iurii. *Sud nad Kievskimi vampirami.* St. Petersburg: Primaia put', 1914.

Bazyler, Michael, and Seth Gerber. "*Chabad v. Russian Federation:* A Case Study in The Use of American Courts to Recover Looted Cultural Property." *International Journal of Cultural Property* 17 (2010): 361–386.

Beilis, Mendel. *The Story of My Sufferings.* New York: The Mendel Beilis Publishing Company, 1926.

Bekhterev, V. M. "The Iushchinskii Murder and the Expert Psychiatric-Psychological Opinion." Translated by Lydia Razran Stone. *Journal of Russian and East European Psychology* 41, no. 2 (2003): 7–70.

Berkowitz, Joel. "The 'Mendel Beilis Epidemic' on the Yiddish Stage." *Jewish Social Studies* 8, no. 1 (2001): 199–225.

Bonch-Bruevich, Vladimir. *Znamenie vremeni: Ubiistvo Andreia Iushchinskogo i delo Beilisa.* Moscow: Gosudarstvennoe izdatel'stvo, 1921.

Brazul'-Brushkovskii, S. I. *Pravda ob ubiistve Iushchinskogo i dele Beilisa.* St. Petersburg, 1913.

Buianov, M. I. *Delo Beilisa.* Moscow: Prometei, 1993.

Calio, Tomasso. "The Cult of the Alleged Ritual Murder Victims in the Second Half of the 20th Century in Italy." In *Ritual Murder: Legend in European History,* Susanna Buttaroni and Musiał Stanisław, eds. Krakow: Association for Cultural Initiatives, 2003.

Carlson, Maria. "Fashionable Occultism: Spiritualism, Theosophy, Freemasonry, and Hermeticism in Fin-de-Siècle Russia." In *The Occult in Russian and Soviet Culture,* Bernice Glotzer Rosenthal, ed. Ithaca, NY: Cornell University Press, 1997.

Chto zhe dal'she? Opravdanie Beilisa i bezpravye evreev. Nice: J. Kleidman, 1914.

Delo Beilisa: Polnyi sudebnyi otchet. Odessa: Odesskii ponedel'nik, 1913.

Dundes, Alan, ed. *The Blood Libel Legend.* Madison: University of Wisconsin Press, 1991.

Elpat'evskii, S. "Sram." *Russkoe bogatstvo* 12 (December 1913): 319–341.

Frankel, Jonathan. *The Damascus Affair: "Ritual Murder," Politics, and the Jews in 1840.* Cambridge, UK: Cambridge University Press, 1997.

Gofshtetter, I. *Ubiistvo Iushchinskogo i russkaia obshchestvennaia sovest'.* St. Petersburg: Novoe vremia, 1914.

Gruzenberg, Oskar. *Yesterday: Memoirs of a Russian-Jewish Lawyer.* Berkeley: University of California Press, 1981.

Hamm, Michael. *Kiev: A Portrait, 1800–1917.* Princeton: Princeton University Press, 1993.

Harris, Ruth. *Dreyfus: Politics, Emotion, and the Scandal of the Century.* New York: Metropolitan Books, 2010.

Hillis, Faith. "Between Empire and Nation: Urban Politics, Community, and Violence in Kiev." PhD dissertation, Yale University, 2010.

Hsia, R. Po-Chia. *The Myth of Ritual Murder: Jews and Magic in Reformation Germany.* New Haven: Yale University Press, 1988.

———. *Trent 1475: Stories of a Ritual Murder Trial.* New Haven: Yale University Press, 1992.

Hutt, Sherry, and David Tarler, eds. *Yearbook of Cultural Property Law 2010.* Walnut Creek, CA: Left Coast Press, 2010.

Katsis, Leonid. *Krovavyi navet i russkaia mysl'.* Moscow: Mosty kul'tury, 2006.

Katz, Jacob. *From Prejudice to Destruction: Antisemitism, 1700–1933.* Cambridge, MA: Harvard University Press, 1980.

Kieff Ritual Murder Accusation: Protests from Leading Christians in Europe. London: Jewish Chronicle and Jewish Tribune, 1913.

Kieval, Hillel. "Death and the Nation: Ritual Murder as Political Discourse in the Czech Lands." *Jewish History* 10, no. 1 (Spring 1996), 75–91.

———. "The Importance of Place: Comparative Aspects of the Ritual Murder Trial in Modern Central Europe." In *Comparing Jewish Societies,* Todd Endelman, ed. Ann Arbor: University of Michigan Press, 1997, 135–165.

———. "Representation and Knowledge in Medieval and Modern Accounts of Jewish Ritual Murder." *Jewish Social Studies: History, Culture, and Society* 1 (Fall 1994), 52–72.

Klier, John. "Cry Blood Murder." *East European Jewish Affairs* 36, no. 2 (December 2006): 213–229.

———. *Imperial Russia's Jewish Question, 1855–1881.* Cambridge, UK: Cambridge University Press, 1995.

———. "The Origins of the 'Blood Libel' in Russia." *Newsletter of the Study Group on Eighteenth-Century Russia* 14 (1986): 12–22.

Klier, John, and Shlomo Lambrozo, eds. *Pogroms: Anti-Jewish Violence in Modern Russian History.* Cambridge, UK: Cambridge University Press, 1992.

Kuras, Ivan. *Sprava Beilisa: pohliad iz s'ohodennia.* Kiev: Instytut natsional'nykh vidnosyn i politolohii NAN Ukraïny, 1994.

Langer, Jack. "Corruption and the Counterrevolution: The Rise and Fall of the Black Hundred." PhD dissertation, Duke University, 2007.

Langmuir, Gavin. *Toward a Definition of Anti-Semitism.* Berkeley: University of California Press, 1990.

Lindemann, Albert. *The Jew Accused: Three Anti-Semitic Affairs (Dreyfus, Beilis, Frank), 1894–1915*. Cambridge, UK: Cambridge University Press, 1991.

Marcus, Jacob. *The Jew in the Medieval World: A Source Book*. Cincinnati: Hebrew Union College Press, 1999.

Margolin, Arnold. *The Jews of Eastern Europe*. New York: T. Seltzer, 1926.

Murav, Harriet. "The Beilis Ritual Murder Trial and the Culture of the Apocalypse." *Cardozo Studies in Law and Literature* 2, no. 2 (2000): 243–263.

Nabokov, Vladimir. "Delo Beilisa." *Pravo* 44 (November 3, 1913): 2519–2524, and 45 (November 10, 1913): 2569–2580.

Nemes, Robert. "Hungary's Antisemitic Provinces: Violence and Ritual Murder in the 1880s." *Slavic Review* 66, no. 1 (Spring 2007), 20–44.

Pavlov, E. *Meditsinskaia ekspertiza po delu Beilisa*. St. Petersburg: Tip. E. F. Meks, 1914.

Petrazhitskii, Leon. "O ritual'nykh ubiistvakh i dele Beilisa." *Pravo* 42 (October 20, 1913): 2403–2423.

Pidzharenko, Aleksandr. *Ne ritual'noe ubiistvo na Luk'ianovke: Kriminal'nyi sysk Kieva V nach XX v.* Kiev: Izd. KVSHCH, 2006.

"Protsess Beilisa v otsenke departamenta politsii." *Krasnyi arkhiv* 44 (1931): 84–125.

Rockaway, Robert, and Arnon Gutfeld. "Demonic Images of the Jew in the Nineteenth Century United States." *American Jewish History* 89, no. 4 (2002): 355–381.

Rogger, Hans. "The Beilis Case: Anti-Semitism and Politics in the Reign of Nicholas II." *Slavic Review* 25, no. 4 (1966): 615–629.

Roth, Cecil, ed., *The Ritual Murder Libel and the Jews*. London: Woburn Press, 1935.

Ruud, Charles, and Sergei Stepanov. *Fontanka 16: The Tsar's Secret Police*. Montreal: McGill-Queen's University Press, 1999.

Samuel, Maurice. *Blood Accusation: The Strange History of the Beilis Case*. New York: Knopf, 1966.

Shulgin, Vasilii. *The Years: Memoirs of a Member of the Russian Duma, 1906–1907*. New York: Hippocrene Books, 1984.

Stepanov, Sergei A. *Chernaia sotnia v Rossii (1905–1914 gg.)*. Moscow: Isd-vo VZPI, 1992.

Strack, Hermann. *Po povodu dela Iushchinskogo i ekspertizy Pranaitisa*. Berlin, 1913.

Tager, Alexander. *The Decay of Czarism: The Beilis Trial*. Philadelphia: Jewish Publication Society of America, 1935.

———. *Tsarskaia Rossiia i delo Beilisa. K istorii antisemitizma*. 2nd revised edition. Moscow: OGIZ, 1934.

Teter, Magda. *Sinners on Trial: Jews and Sacrilege after the Reformation*. Cambridge, MA: Harvard University Press, 2011.

Trachtenberg, Joshua. *The Devil and the Jews: The Medieval Conception of the Jew and Its Relation to Modern Antisemitism*. New Haven: Yale University Press, 1943.

"Tsarskaia pravitel'stvo i protsess Beilisa." *Krasnyi arkhiv* 54–55 (1932): 162–204.

Ubiistvo Iushchinskogo: Mnenia inostrannykh uchenykh. St. Petersburg, 1913.

Walser Smith, Helmut. *The Butcher's Tale: Murder and Anti-Semitism in a German Town.* New York: W. W. Norton, 2002.

Weinberg, Robert. "Popular Antisemitism and the Occult in Late Imperial Russia: Ritual Murder and the Trial of Mendel Beilis." In *Russia's Century of Revolutions: Parties, People, and Places,* Michael Melancon and Donald Raleigh, eds. Bloomington: Indiana University Press, 2012, 17–35.

Weinberg, Robert. "Look! Up There in the Sky: It's a Vulture, It's a Bat . . . It's a Jew: Reflections on Antisemitism in Late Imperial Russia, 1906–1914." In *Jews in the East European Borderlands: Daily Life, Violence, and Memory,* Eugene Avrutin and Harriet Murav, eds. Brighton, MA: Academic Studies Press, 2012, 167–186.

Index

Robert Weinberg is Professor of History at Swarthmore College and author of *The Revolution of 1905 in Odessa: Blood on the Steps* (IUP, 1993) and *Stalin's Forgotten Zion: Birobidzhan and the Making of a Soviet Jewish Homeland.*

CPSIA information can be obtained at www.ICGtesting.com
Printed in the USA
BVOW07s1326061113

335618BV00002B/2/P

9 780253 011077